W-3

A MEMOIR

W-3

BETTE
HOWLAND

INTRODUCTION BY YIYUN LI

A PUBLIC SPACE BOOKS

A Public Space Books
PO Box B
New York, NY 10159

First published by The Viking Press, 1974
First A Public Space Books edition, 2021

A Public Space gratefully acknowledges the generous support of the
Drue and H. J. Heinz II Charitable Trust, the Chisholm Foundation, the
National Endowment for the Arts, the New York State Council on the Arts,
the Amazon Literary Partnership, and the corporations, foundations, and
individuals whose contributions have helped to make this book possible.

Library of Congress Control Number: 2019905772
ISBN   978-0-9982675-3-1
eISBN 978-1-7339730-5-2
Distributed by Publishers Group West

apublicspace.org

9 8 7 6 5 4 3 2 1

INTRODUCTION

Yiyun Li

A few years ago, before I left a psychiatric hospital in New York, the doctor who signed off on my release said to me, "You can write about your time here as long as you don't name the hospital." How mad, I thought then, would I have to be to write about this. What *this* was I didn't want to articulate. I had set my heart to not remember, which, to my mind, was different from forgetting. To forget would be a disloyalty to my profession. To not remember felt like a necessity for writing, and for living.

Reading *W-3*, Bette Howland's memoir about her stay in a Chicago psychiatric ward, I had a sense of reliving memory. Temporal and geographical settings matter little in the eternal struggle between lucidity and lunacy. The characters in *W-3* could be the same people I encountered in S-6, the ward where I stayed: the loquacious and the wordless; the violent and the frozen; those who believed themselves to be unfairly locked up and those who celebrated their readmissions with fanfare. The unmistakable divides: Between races and classes. Where a patient came from and would return to—New York City or the suburbs, Manhattan or the other boroughs, an African American neighborhood or a Haitian American neighborhood in Brooklyn, a homeless shelter or a halfway home or one with a secure and private roof.

Another patient told me that every one of us had a book to write after leaving the hospital. Call it "Woman, Interrupted," she said. No one, I thought, would be omniscient enough, lucid enough, selfless enough to write that book. What is in one's possession contains one's blind spot: luck, suffering, desire, misgiving; the wish to rewrite, revise, restart a life; the wish to withdraw and to depart. And, of course, our egos, vulnerable and recalcitrant. Preoccupied with our individual concerns, we forget that we are not that different from one another. "That was the trouble. There was no novelty. One gesture was stale, powerless, and unoriginal as the next. Nothing was original on W-3," Howland writes. "That was its truth and beauty."

Bette Howland wrote a book that I thought was impossible to write. Less personal than a conventional memoir—Howland herself occupies minimal space—it can be read as an encyclopedia of life in a psychiatric ward, written from within a mental turmoil yet with preternatural omniscience. Can a single entry, a single life, contain the entire encyclopedia? It is a preposterous question, but an exceptional book warrants questioning the improbable and the impossible.

The best writing often grants the reader a new way to understand a narrative, a situation, a moment, even individual words. I am not so naive as to forget the politics of language, but reading *W-3*, I found myself thinking about two words in other than their usual settings.

Refugee/refuge: their Latin root is *fugere*, to flee; *re-* indicates a backward intention, to flee back.

Dissident: the Latin root is *dis-* + *sedēre*, to sit apart, to disagree.

Anyone in a psychiatric hospital could be called a refugee. One person's reason for fleeing the world is not that different from another's. The border between the unresolvable and unlivable is not clearly marked; often one crosses it before knowing it. *W-3* starts when Bette Howland has already crossed the border and become a reluctant refugee. To flee backward is instinct, though back to what, one has no way to articulate. "What was I?" Howland writes. "It seemed to me that I was standing on the threshold of two worlds, and neither was particularly desirable."

When I was in the hospital, a few patients had the idea of having a talent show on a Saturday—a change from bingo playing and *Jeopardy!* watching and endless waiting. An orphan, nineteen years old, who had been homeless for months, rehearsed on the piano nonstop—she was a good pianist. A veteran who could barely leave her room sang "Amazing Grace" all day long, with different patients stopping by to practice with her. *Community*—as Howland portrays it—is a ubiquitous word that insists on how everyone should live in W-3 or S-6, outside of everyday life yet loyally imitating the life outside. Community is what life is, unless, of course, one resists: to disagree, to sit apart.

Different people tried to get me to participate in the talent show. The young pianist placed her hands on my ribs and asked me to say *Ahhh*, explaining how to project from the diaphragm. Alas, I have no talents to offer, I said, but an audience member's appreciation. I was not being entirely genuine. I was a staunch yet indifferent dissident, which I believe marks the difference between Howland and me. She was a dissident too, sitting apart, but she was also sitting very close, the distance between her and the W-3 community nearly imperceptible. In this book she presents little disagreement with herself or her community. Was there disagreement at all? Her position seems to me ambivalent: there she is, a resident and a dissident. Neither position entirely desirable, she nevertheless moves from one to the other with chameleonic ease. Perhaps that is why she could write this impossible book. A pure dissident is reactive; a pure resident loses perspective.

W-3 was Bette Howland's first book, published in 1974. She published two more books, won a MacArthur Fellowship, then disappeared from public attention. In 2015, when Brigid Hughes of *A Public Space* found a copy in the one-dollar bin at a secondhand bookstore, her work had long been out of print and forgotten. I often think about those years, and I wonder if this book offers some clues. Howland is a dissident in W-3. Was Howland the writer a dissident in life too, not in opposition to any regime or politics but to defy expectations, which she would have known how to meet (had she wanted that for her career)? Her guiding principle seems to have been simply to observe. I have often equated willfulness with a wish to negate or to propel, though Howland's willfulness feels neutral: to watch the world in such an attentive way that through observing, the writer can nearly free herself from her blind spot. Nearly, yet never entirely—the latter would be the biggest blind spot of all.

But the world often prizes digestible narratives and claimable positions, and blind spots are sometimes granted privileges above perceptions. To bring Bette Howland's work back to the public is a reminder that observing and remembering are not passive but intensely and inwardly active.

W-3

I.

In the intensive care unit there was a woman who had undergone open-heart surgery. A monitor was implanted in her heart; it beeped every second of the day and night, a persistent tempo, never racing or slowing down as a human heart seems to, unaccountable times on the most ordinary days of our lives. If it had, the nurses would have been there on the double, their brisk white heels disappearing behind the swaying curtains. The woman was unconscious, she had never come out of it; her life was just a mechanism—its regular pace audible all through the ward.

I must have been hearing this beeping sound for a long time before I knew it.

I was struck later by the opening words of an essay a blind girl wrote about blindness: "It must be dark. That's what people always say to you. But it isn't dark. It isn't anything." Maybe I am wrong about this, but before all this it wasn't dark—it wasn't anything. And it could have taken any amount of time to come to the surface, to reach the threshold of confusion. There was a vague, struggling sort of pain and a briny taste—the flavor of seawater. (This was the vapor of a breathing machine.) My consciousness seemed to be fixed, leveled, on a peculiar penetrating announcement:

BEEP...BEEP...BEEP...

"It's all right now. You're going to be all right." Someone was whispering in my ear. "It's all over now, it's all behind you. You will start life anew." *Anew*, the voice said. "You will be reborn."

I couldn't see anything.

None of this seemed strange to me; I did not have the energy for such reflections. At this time I had no thoughts of my own, no emotions. The only real stimulus was pain, and I couldn't figure out exactly where it was coming from. I was flat—strictly out of commission. Both hands were weighted down, taped to boards and pinned to tubes (they felt like oars); both ankles too. There was a rawness around the anus and urethra—more tubes, I reckoned from past experience. The tubes that had run down my mouth and nose I had ripped out myself in some bout of semiconsciousness. These tubes were now my greatest preoccupation; it seemed to me that they were tying me up, cutting me off, tangling my life—I wanted to get free. I kept struggling to lift my head and snap at them—clicking my teeth, wanting to bite them in two.

"You are reborn!" my mother was whispering. She had been waiting three days, camped in hospital corridors and waiting rooms, for me to wake up. Did she plan what she was going to say? Or had it come to her only at this moment? I never asked, although I know what she was trying to do. In her own way she was reviving me, resuscitating me—like all those machines, masks, needles, tubes she saw sticking out of me everywhere. But it was that other system she was feeding, the most vital life function. She was a mother after all, I was her daughter; she belonged to that system. And I had repudiated it. So now she was trying to set it going again.

Reborn. Anew. BEEP…BEEP…BEEP…

I had not known that such words lay so close to the surface, on the tip of the tongue. For a long time they had been my deepest secret, my protectors, my closest companions. And it surprised me now, to hear them repeated aloud in this way. So they were no secret after all. There was nothing special about them. They didn't even belong to me—evidently they were common property. The first feeling I experienced, then, in the first few moments of this, my new life, was a dim sense of disappointment. My desires seemed lacking, shopworn, powerless, passionless.

But the shortcomings of a previous existence did not have much hold on me now, couldn't compete with the one thing that vividly concerned me—the tubes. I heard myself begging for them to be taken away.

At that time I had no voice, could speak only in a vehemently inaudible whisper. The vocal cords got stretched out by the tubes that had run through the nostrils, down the trachea; the voice was a sort of hoarse vapor. I spoke with a will, but nothing came out. This was one of the things that happens. There were other things. The coughing machine for instance, a rackety apparatus; violent activity, the equivalent of swimming a choppy channel. It had been with me twenty minutes out of every hour of the day and night, the first thing I had become aware of, and now one of the strange but primary facts of my life. I had vomited, as people who take a massive overdose of sleeping pills are apt to do, and the matter had been sucked and swallowed into my lungs; I was being dredged out. These were the—unanticipated—physiological facts.

The intensive care unit was never dark; it was lit at all times, day and night, a kind of steady, unremitting brightness that seemed to belong to the same category of things as the beeping signal. My bed seemed moored in the midst of the large, gleaming room. One of the nurses was a big police-matron type with great thick officious forearms and a bosom to match; muscularity—not made for tenderness. For hammerlocks, maybe; for carving bread on. Once, as that starched bib bustled about the room, I called out to her repeatedly. I was in pain. My voice was inaudible, and she didn't seem to hear me. I tried to catch her eye. Couldn't she see my mouth was open?

At last she disappeared behind the curtains.

Two cleaning women—the inevitable thin black figures in dark blue uniforms who would become such a familiar sight when I got to W-3—were pushing mops across the floor. They saw my predicament and glanced at each other; one laid down her mop and went over to the curtains. By now I was watching those curtains with all my might. The woman came back, picked up her mop: "I told her you was calling," she said, thrusting and shoving, not raising her eyes to my face. "But she say she can't hear you."

"Fucking bitch," I whispered at the curtains.

Instantly they parted; muscular arms slung them aside with a ring: *"What did you call me?"*

In defense of the nurse I must admit that such outcries went on all the time and did not seem especially expressive or moving to me either. For the sick in their beds were invisible. They were only there by implication. They must have existed, if only for the sake of this other life, full of importance—the bustling arms, starched coats; the carts, mops, ringings, beepings; the brisk comings and goings of white-stockinged nurses.

The hospital was a teaching institution; the corridors teemed with lively packs of medical students. Several times a day, classes would come trooping in—the hems of their white coats energetically flapping—and rank themselves, behind their professor, round the foot of my bed.

"Do you know your name? Do you know where you are?" the professor would ask, leaning over the side bar. What did they want from me? Surely not the answers to such questions.

"Do you know what time it is?"

That was a stumper. A room without darkness or daylight, the same lights burning night and day. I received no meals; the coughing machine came round the clock. The heart patient's monitor beeped every second, without reference to the hour. A burned man cried out under sedation: there was nothing in his screams and groans to suggest the passage of time.

The professor noticed my hesitation, and his glance slid toward his students. Their coats were so stiff and straight, their mustaches and beards had such dark, silky intensity, that it startled me to see how bored were the faces behind them. Glazed eyes, cheeks like bricks, stifling their yawns. *Did you catch that? She doesn't know what time it is.*

He urged me to take a guess. By now of course he would be whispering intimately. It was on account of my voice; people couldn't help whispering.

I never saw the woman who lay behind the curtains, and that seems strange to me; the beeping of her heart pervaded my life. It seemed to generate a great deal of traffic too. The woman's sisters, dressed in black, with large handbags slung over their elbows and exposed, white, freckled arms, went to and fro on tiptoe. There is a whole subculture attached to these intensive care units, the relatives who post themselves outside in waiting rooms, man their stations. It's a strange sort of peripheral life, an offstage life. But patients themselves don't know about it, don't know what goes on out there; they are not aware of all this waiting. They are seldom aware of one another.

Actually the intensive care unit was filled at all times with noises, the outcries and agonies of the patients—though nothing else so unrelenting as the beeping. The burned man yelled. He had been in an industrial accident, a chemical flash fire; his screams were like muscle contractions. Behind another partition a girl rotated; this had something to do with an open wound in her stomach. No—she was fixed; it was the bed that moved around her, changing her position, and all the while a powerful arc lamp, like a searchlight, irradiated the wound. I imagined this arrangement as something like a Ferris wheel, with smoking, sweeping lights. I never saw her either. I never saw anybody. I knew of these details, of the very existence of these others, only from my mother, who had spent all that time in the waiting room stationed outside the swinging doors.

Every time the doors swept open my mother would raise her handsome, conspicuous white head—sleek, striking, like an ermine; terribly alert—ready to jump up and start asking questions. She knew herself these questions were of no use, but she couldn't help asking, petitioning. Adaptable, resourceful, persistent (the eternal curses of human nature—but above all persistent), she had napped in the waiting room, under her coat, had grabbed her meals in the cafeteria, had rinsed her teeth in the john. In other words, she had established a life of sorts, a routine of her own, with its own habits and rules and even her own set of acquaintances—people in the same circumstances. Since the actual business of life, the visits, occupied only five minutes out of every hour, there was plenty of time left for striking up acquaintances. And my mother, a notoriously sociable type, couldn't drift down to the lobby in an elevator without starting a conversation with strangers.

So she was friendly with the sisters of the heart patient, and especially with the parents of the golden-haired girl on the rack (she described the lovely hair). And before that—the casualty rate being what it was here—with the father of a Chinese boy who had a rare heart condition. In the midst of the waiting room, the saloon doors burst open and the boy was wheeled out past their eyes to surgery. His heart under the white sheet seemed violently possessed—active, jumping like a frog, my mother told me. And the tears stood out in the father's eyes. The boy had died before I came to.

I wouldn't even have known what the beeping of the heart monitor was (it seemed natural enough, the pulse of the room—the fluttering air vents were its breath) if my mother had not explained it all to me. Naturally, since it was forbidden, she had peeked through the curtains and seen the woman—a battered body, black and blue all over like a tattooed lady. There was something weird in her depictions—bizarre, racy, freakish, like a street carnival, a sideshow, a circus. It made a vivid and peculiar impression on me; maybe it was my weakened condition. The vitality of these particular individual details is powerful medicine; and these were strong doses.

It was no surprise to find myself in a hospital bed, because I had spent a lot of time in hospitals lately; had been sick on and off for a long time—various mysterious physical ailments, finally diagnosed as a kidney infection. (This would become a familiar story later on when I got to W-3; not only did most inmates have such a history of physical depletion, long debilitating sickness, but "kidney infection" turned out to be one of the most common complaints. After I heard this a few times, I began to understand.)

The first time, many months before, I had been in a hospital clear on the other side of the city—quite a different place, very small and dingy. A hole in the wall. It partook of the general gloom of the neighborhood, a poor Puerto Rican district—grimy bricks, neon pipes, broken glass. And the emergency room of this little hospital had a reputation; this was where the cops would haul you into if you got pinched, drunk and disorderly and needing medical attention. My uncle was a cop on this beat and he told me how battered victims, with eyes sealed shut and the blood trickling down their cheeks, would beg the police officers and try to bribe them to be taken to some other place.

"Anywhere else—not there! Not that hospital! I got money in my pants at home!" they'd say.

I was only in that hospital for "tests." (If only they could find something "wrong" with me.) Down the hall there had been a patient experiencing the rapid course of a raging communicable disease. The doctors put on disposable paper uniforms when they had business in that room, and everything—masks, caps, rubber gloves—had to be burned immediately afterward. Visitors peered through a thickly shielded window, hardly more than a peephole. Most of the other patients seemed to be in the restaurant trade (the hospital evidently had some sort of deal with the union insurance)—Puerto Rican dishwashers, Greek busboys in traction, chefs, cocktail waitresses with saffron-tinted eyeballs, symptoms of hepatitis and yellow jaundice. In the bathroom I saw old foreign women, Polish, Slavic, Lithuanian, limping painfully about the open stalls, bare backed in their string-tied gowns. Hotel maids probably, washroom matrons. The irony was that the john was such a grisly place—filthy, smeared with feces, and they spent their lives cleaning up such messes. In fact the whole hospital was indescribably demoralizing, dreary, straight out of the nineteenth century. Blackened walls, peeling paint, iron-barred beds; no one thrust a broom into these dark corners.

Only the precautions concerning the quarantined mystery patient had seemed sterilized, efficient, up to date.

Who this was, whether male or female, I did not know. A succession of visitors passed my door; I could always tell which ones they were. They were black—and they were beautiful. To the extreme. Extremely tall, extremely thin, dressed in the bizarre height of elegance—feathers, turbans, silks and skins, lashes thick as horsehair—like illustrations in Paris *Vogue*. Their perfect, expressionless, mannequin faces showed no emotion; but sometimes I woke in the night and saw them pacing up and down in the dismal-lighted corridors.

Who was it? Who was in there? Who was receiving such homage? That's what I had wanted to ask them.

This went on for two or three days. Then late one afternoon on my way to the bathroom I saw two masked men in green paper uniforms, with rubber aprons and rubber gloves, scurrying along, stooping and dragging a long sealed bundle of black vinyl. Their arms were flailing; their heels rapidly tapping. No one else was around; the corridor must have been cleared for this purpose. I realized that this was the mystery patient.

I thought of this black bundle often now.

As soon as I was well enough to leave intensive care, I was transferred to another ward on another floor of the hospital. I was not strong enough yet for the stimulation of life on W-3. In fact I did not know yet that they had such plans for me.

It was an ordinary semiprivate room. Here however I had to have private nurses round the clock, a rule of the hospital; I might still be despondent, disposed to harm myself; it was a matter of surveillance. Are you going to try that again? The question was put to me. How is your mood? Such inquiries are routine with attempted suicides, but they made no sense at all to me. I was weak, feeble; my voice was less than a whisper. Here I sipped yellow chicken broth and peed warm yellow pee into chilly bedpans—an improvement over being fed through needles and drained through tubes—but the results were essentially the same. Nothing left over.

I had no "mood," that is to say, no surplus.

Nothing was wasted; everything that left the body was reserved and measured. This included the stuff I spat into the plastic cup of the coughing machine. There were two parts to this procedure: first you inhaled the vapor through a mask, breathing deeper and deeper; the vapor loosened the matter in the lungs, rattled it, you broke into a sweat from the effort.

Then you had to suck the briny steam through a tube, and this brought on the coughing. Fits. Spasms. It was uncontrollable. My eyes squeezed tears, my chest hacked away at its inner darkness. Meantime the pump was visibly agitating the water—in the little clear tank I could see it foaming and churning.

After the violent, raging preliminaries, the end product— the cough itself—seemed fragile, a disappointment. Each blast brought up very little, barely enough worth spitting. At the end of twenty minutes of effort, there might be a tablespoonful of alien, life-threatening matter in the little plastic cup.

While such a session was going on—it naturally consumed my attention—I was aware that someone else had come into the room, stealing quietly about on her white crepe soles. She was a tall, handsome, glossy-haired black woman with sweater sleeves dangling from the shoulders of her uniform. This must be Henrietta, the private nurse who would stay with me through the night—I saw her picking up my chart. It was already thick. She sat down and curled her legs up in the armchair, riffling the pages in her lap; shrugging and clutching at the neck of her sweater. So it was cold in the room? I couldn't tell, I was always too cold.

All at once something caught her eye and she shot a quick sharp glance at me. She turned the chart over, smoothing out its pages, and began to read again from the beginning—this time more intently, her fist at her throat. And I could feel her eyes lifting and lighting on me each time she folded back a page. So I could tell that she was reading all about me; that is to say, what I had done, for at that time (and for some time after) that was the primary fact about me.

I would like to put this in a recognizable form. For a long time it had seemed to me that life was about to begin—real life. But there was always some obstacle in the way. Something to be got through first, some unfinished business; time still to be served, a debt to be paid. Then life could begin. At last it had dawned on me that these obstacles were my life. I was always rolling these stones from my grave.

These last weeks I had been alone in my apartment, packing up. I had spent the summer months in the hospital, flat on my back; had lost my job, my two sons were staying with relatives. Then a large hand reached out—grabbed me by the scruff of the neck, scooped me up: I was notified of a grant from a foundation to finish a book. We were moving again—we moved very often—this time to a better climate, for our health. Our old flat was bare, dark, curtainless now, the windows gloomy with their long, torn paper shades.

The walls were thin; my neighbor laughed and talked loudly to himself and I knew that things were not right with him. Sometimes he delivered speeches, pacing up and down, and he sang John Philip Sousa marches in the john: Be *kind* to your web-footed *friends. Quack quack* down the bathtub drain. A big, round, bully sort of fellow. He looked a little like Moby-Dick: walleyes, fishy white hands. But when I heard him stumbling home from Walgreens, whistling, with the bottles jostling and clinking in his shopping bag, I knew that I was in for it.

"Greaseball! Nigger! Kike!" he would begin to bellow through the walls—this was for me, I'm very dark. "Cunt!"— through his teeth. He dared me to come out, he would show me a thing or two. Drunk, crashing about the room and punching the walls.

I wanted to beat on my walls with bare fists. Stop it! Leave me alone! I was terrified of him, I hated him, I wished he could be murdered or run down in the street. And yet a man's home is his castle.

At that time stranger things had started happening to me. I was discovering that I couldn't sleep. The nights were hot and stormy, unseasonable, the tattered window shades twisted and rattled. Morbid thoughts overtook me; they flocked to my bed unbidden. I dreamed of strange, vivid acts: the squint of razor blades digging and sawing my wrists. Something I knew I could never go through with—too squeamish—and yet I went over the exercise repeatedly: saw myself wincing, determined, spiteful, blinking, biting my lip. For the first time in my life—I had always been afraid of them, afraid, I suppose, of sudden impulses—I got a prescription for sleeping pills. Thoughts of suicide had become constant; I dragged them around like a weight. In my thick, drugged sleep it was the same, a ball and chain; an incubus visited me, I felt its numb pressure beside me on the bed, holding down the bedclothes. It rolled on top of me. I had a fantasy: I would be smothered in the act of fellatio with the devil.

This was when I began to see myself rising from bed, trotting past the packing boxes (grocery cartons, liquor crates) to the bathroom with its ancient grout and missing tiles—the little hexagonal kind we used to use for laggers playing hop-scotch. Opening the medicine cabinet (now here's a curiosity: Why the medicine cabinet? The pills were actually right beside my bed. But never mind, it seems there has to be a medicine cabinet, fantasy must have its way) and fishing for the little bottle behind the silver mirror. I would turn the handle of the faucet, the water would gush full force… But the days passed, the supply of pills was dwindling; seven, six, five—not enough.

I tried to talk myself out of it. Indeed, my mind was full of noble thoughts, always preoccupied with the loftiest sentiments about life and why it ought to be continued. (I needed an excuse!) It was like trying to move with artificial limbs. I refilled the prescription and swallowed all the pills.

One thing surprised me. Dying was not what I had expected; it wasn't anything like what I had imagined it would be all those times I'd gone over it in my head, stretched out in the dark as if awaiting its approach. And I thought I knew it so well. I pretty quickly regretted what I had done and called the doctor; he couldn't be reached. I told the voice of the answering service what had happened and sat down and waited for him to return the call. That was all. Nothing happened. No stealth, no reckoning; no leaden weight; it didn't start with the feet, creep up the legs. My mind went out first, blew like a fuse. Evidently I had gotten undressed, a creature of habit, and lain down between the sheets in an orderly fashion. I never heard the telephone. But I had later learned that someone rang the bell, that I had spoken with him through the black mouthpiece by the door buzzer in a sluggish, sullen voice, and he had gone away wondering what was wrong. I had no recollection of this at all, I have never remembered it; it was just as if no one was home.

The doctor got no answer and called the police.

The coughing machine had been rolled away on its soft rubber feet; the corridor was dim and quiet. The other bed in my room was empty—its occupant had been removed quite suddenly, taken down for surgery. "But I was just fixing to have my dinner!" she complained. A lively, sharp-tongued black woman. It was true; she was sitting cranked up in bed, her tray spread out before her, shaking the silverware out of her napkin. I was watching all this with such keen interest because I was gnawingly hungry and wasn't getting anything to eat. She kept on scolding—letting everyone have it—as they pulled the cotton stockings over her feet, tucked the surgical cap about her head so that her ears stuck out. "Is the scar going to show in my bikini?" She had told me that she had six grandchildren.

But all this must have been hours before; suddenly I was worried about her. Her bed had been prepared, postsurgical; the smooth, flat white sheet glared under the bed lamp. Why hadn't she come back?

A strange thing was happening. It was the first in some days I had had a specific sense of time, its passing. In intensive care, no time prevailed, it was all the same. Now I was aware of the late hour, certain of it; an odd sensation—we had moved deep into night. Darkness was plastered against the window. Only the bed lamp was burning; the sensible, self-conserving Henrietta was reading in a very bad light.

"Now," she said. And she rose and came over and sidled up onto the foot of my bed. She was silent for a moment, regarding me coolly from a distance with her fawn-colored eyes; one hand on her hip, the other clasping her throat.

"Now, you're much too young, too pretty a girl, to have tried a thing like that," she began, pursing her lips and shutting her eyes. She shook her throat at me. "Now, that won't do at all," she said.

I understood that Henrietta had made up her mind to give me a pep talk. It went something like this:

Everybody has their problems, nobody's perfect. You're nothing special, this *whole world*'s a mess. Nothing *you* can do about it. You can't let it bother you, you have to learn to live with it, have to make up your mind. "That's what I did," she said.

Now, take Henrietta's husband—he was bossy. "I'm not saying it against the man—a fact's a fact. Nothing he can do about it." Her husband was an automobile mechanic but he preached in their church on Sundays, and Henrietta was very proud of him; he was some preacher. The trouble was, as the week progressed, got closer and closer to Sunday, the man got bossier and bossier. He started in practicing on everybody, preaching at them right and left. "He gets so touchy, ain't nobody can come near him; you can hear him carrying on all over the house." Henrietta used to let it bother her, but she had learned to *live with* it, she had *made* up her *mind*; now she just went upstairs and shut the door. By Saturday night her husband was a *hard* man to live with, but on Monday morning he was meek as a lamb. "He gets it all out of his system," she said.

"Now take my daughter—*she* is *cold*." Henrietta was the first to admit it, the girl was unusual that way. "I tell her myself, 'Girl, *you* are *cold*!'" She shuddered and caught at her sweater with its loose, dangling sleeves. "But she better learn to live with it," Henrietta quickly added. The daughter had a most surprising ambition, she wanted to go to mortician's school. Henrietta had her misgivings: "There aren't many women in the field," she told me. But there have to be undertakers in the world, and it may as well be someone like that—"She won't let it bother her." Anyway, the girl had *made* up her *mind*. She knew her own nature, peculiarly cold-blooded as that might be. "She may not be all that bright, but is she stubborn!" Henrietta shuddered again. "I won't stand in her way."

I watched Henrietta as she talked; who could help watching her? She was fascinating, overpowering. A strong, beautiful woman, her hair clinging to her like an animal's coat. And she seemed to be growing all the while, becoming more and more intense, gathering her forces together—dragging and clutching at her sweater, with her hand at her throat. I felt diminished in this powerful presence.

The way I saw it, Henrietta had good reason to be satisfied. A preacher, a nurse, and an undertaker—what more could you ask for? They'd have us coming and going. Body and soul, sickness and health, this world and the next—it was all sewed up.

But something was wrong. Henrietta pursed her lips, looking at me intently; her eyes so much lighter than her skin. She was not getting her message across, not getting through to me. I seemed too passive, inert, as I lay cowering under my many blankets. My hair had been shorn very short—fleeçed like a sheep.

I had hardly said a word the whole time, and it finally struck her. She edged off the bed and came and stood beside my pillow. "Your voice," she said suspiciously. "What's the matter with your voice?"

I explained in a feeble whisper.

This was the opportunity she had been waiting for.

"Now, you've got that all wrong, it's all in your head," she said. There was absolutely nothing the matter with my voice; Henrietta was a nurse and she ought to know. I couldn't talk because I had talked myself into it—and she was going to see to it that I talked myself out. Right now. "You're going to make up your mind."

Henrietta commanded me to sit. She propped up my pillows and cranked the bed upright under me. "Now take a deep breath," she told me, standing back and watching with her elbows crossed under her sleeves.

I sat up stiffly, hunched my shoulders, sucked in my breath.

"Now say ah!"

"*Ah*," I whispered.

Henrietta shook her head. "Take a deep breath, I said— Deep! Deep! Deeper—from here." She placed one hand beneath her breast and swelled like an opera singer. Her face, with its broad, distended nostrils, grew dark and grim.

"Ahhh!" she said at last, explosively.

"*Ahhh*," I gasped, sticking out my cropped head.

Henrietta clicked her tongue. "I don't know what we're going to do with you," she said.

I didn't know why I had no voice and I didn't really care—didn't have the energy to talk. I know now that it was impossible for me to produce a normal sound, just as if I had no vocal cords; but I didn't know it then, didn't know but what Henrietta might be right. And I was too weak, too intimidated, to resist her. My coughing machine would not return for four hours—the first time I was having such a respite—but this was like a session with the coughing machine. I pitched forward from the pillows, heaved my shoulders, clutched my throat—nothing came out. My throat was raveled, I had no forces to gather.

I don't know how long this went on. Who is it has the dream that eternity is a spider? He is alone in a room with a great hairy-legged spider.

Later Henrietta tucked her long legs under her in the armchair and dozed off with her sweater round her chin. I was wide awake. I was cold; the empty bed gleamed white under the bed lamp. (It was not until sometime the next day that I learned my roommate had merely been transferred to another ward after surgery.)

It may seem strange, but I wasn't at all curious about what was on that chart Henrietta had been browsing over in her lap. At least that was one form that I had not had to fill out. It seemed to me that I had already filled out too many forms in my time, that I was always filling out forms, making endless applications of one sort or another—jobs, schools, loans, leases—and I hated it, hated completing the blanks, scribbling in dates, hated giving any account of myself. I was sick to death of the facts of my life.

When my mother heard that these private nurses were costing me thirty-five dollars per eight-hour shift, she volunteered at once—characteristically, in order to save me money—to take the day shift. I wasn't too happy about the expense, either. But the thought of spending eight hours alone with my mother, lying helplessly on my back, made my blood run colder. We hadn't spent so much time together in as many years. It was too late however; she had already done battle with the hospital administrators, made a few scenes. It had gotten to the point where it was embarrassing.

But for her I really had been "reborn," I was helpless again, she felt I needed her. The situation was only temporary—she had to make the most of it.

A team of four doctors, three interns and a resident, had been following my case ever since the emergency room. They went everywhere together, seemingly inseparable, marching in with the prongs of their stethoscopes jutting from their pockets and the little hospital dispatch radios beeping on their chests. Dr. Zimbler had great thick bushy muttonchops on his cheeks, so bristling they actually seemed to precede him (he himself usually a few steps ahead of everybody else; an alert, stocky, forthright man). And Dr. Joy, Dr. Scott, Dr. Wax—his sidekicks—ganged up eagerly behind him. By now the doctors were familiar with my mother, who had all this time been so very much in evidence. It was plain that they took her for a sort of archetype of the Possessive Mother, overprotective, meddling, ruining her children's lives. They no longer attempted to conceal it. Whenever they appeared, they drove her out of the room.

"Would you please leave us alone with your daughter now? Would you please stop interfering? Would you please—just for once—let her answer for herself?"

The three young interns stood there, glowering at her, their arms folded across rows of pen clips; Dr. Zimbler put his hands behind his back and paced up and down—thrusting out his muttonchops—waiting for her to leave.

"But she can't talk," my mother replied, in her plausible way. Oh well! Gathering herself up with ruffled dignity, doing her best to seem offended. She certainly could play the part. Noble features; the costly looking Florida tan, the white hair elegant as a powdered wig. Her fine carriage seemed overconfident, overbearing. All was vainglorious. But she was used to being where she was not wanted; it was, you might say, one of her specialties.

She knew I was not pleased that she had come up from Florida to be with me. My father had recently retired from factory work, and my parents had become caretakers on a small Gulf Coast estate. I felt sorry, they did not have to live in this way. They had a bundle—saved with what sweat of the brow, what humiliating efforts, I ought to know—and they could easily have afforded a place in Florida of their own. It was simply force of habit, the habit apparently which had kept them together. Her attractive, bold-checked suit—the slim skirt, boxy jacket looked so aggressively smart on her—was a hand me down from the woman she worked for. My mother would never have bought anything so smart and expensive for herself. She would never have bought anything for herself period, except for her dime-store rings, clustered like grapes on her fingers.

Her large, ringed hands, tight fisted, stalling, defenseless, clutched her purse. I knew the contents by heart, the perfume of her dark lipsticks, minty chewing gum.

At the door, her back halted instinctively. "Then why is she always so cold?" my mother asked, as if wondering out loud, talking to herself—but turning to confront the doctors with stubborn intentions.

"People who take massive doses of poison get cold," the tall intern said, brutally impatient with her. "That's how it is."

It was like a slap in the face. Yes, she had waited in vain for the rewards of motherhood.

We exchanged a smile of grim, dark-eyed complicity. I also knew this look by heart: *You see what a mistake they are making (it said). They don't know that you don't want me here any more than they do. They think that we're like other mothers and daughters, that we're too close, that I have too much power over you. Well I just wish it were so! What's wrong with that, would there be so much harm in it? We have to put up with it though. You won't let on, will you?*

She was actually flattered by the doctors' opinion of her, crudely as it was expressed. She knew this was the closest she was ever going to come to being the "mother" they were ordering out of the room.

I was not about to let on, give her away. I did not want to embarrass my mother.

And yet of course I was an embarrassment, I have always been an embarrassment. And our family life had always seemed to me to consist mainly of stratagems, concealments—how to cover up a series of scandalous facts.

Talk about locking the barn door after the horse is stolen.

"So-and-so is so upset," a typical conversation with my mother might go—naming one of her numerous acquaintances. "She doesn't know what to do. Her son is running around with a divorcée. Serious, he wants to get married. Such a nice boy—and she's older than him and has two kids already."

Now I was a "divorcée" with two small children. I had good reason to appreciate what that lurid word really meant. I knew that benighted condition. A dingy flat, crummy job, constant money worries. Everything you earn goes to doctors and babysitters. Then the baby's got a runny nose, the sitter doesn't show, you can't go to work. A life full of reproaches, self-hatred; a woman supporting a manless (unconsoled) existence, beside herself with fear, worry, managing alone.

So powerful was the force of my mother's disapproval, however, so strong and accustomed its hold on me, that I would immediately see this other divorcée—this fellow creature and sufferer like myself—as a scarlet fallen woman. Taffeta skirts, rhinestone earrings, oily red lips, ankle straps—the works. Clicking castanets, like Carmen! At the same time I would also be wondering where she had managed to find someone who was "serious" about her and wanted to marry her. That was certainly a preoccupation of mine.

One of these flaming creatures had in fact tended me one night in the hospital as my private nurse: a fat, homely, weary young woman on squeaky wedgies, telling me of her troubles while she gave me an enema—my knees doubled up. Her husband had run out on her, left her with an infant. She worked at night because it simplified matters; too hard to get sitters in the daytime. (Nerve-racking business, I knew.) Of course she never went anywhere anymore, never stepped out, never had any fun. She couldn't afford it herself, never got a chance to meet anyone. It was all work and looking after the baby, aggravation about fevers and colds and arranging for sitters, worrying about making ends meet. And bitterly missing out on life.

This last she did not have to add—I could hear her sighing behind me, her heart as heavy as she was.

It was impossible for me to have such a simple, unburdening conversation with my mother. All was mined, booby trapped; all was concealment. Of course I had to understand that for her I myself was that notorious figure, the trampish divorcée, the mantrap. This was very far from the truth—maybe too far. My life was much like that nurse's; and the deficiencies of such a life were in the forefront of my mind.

How to discuss the particulars? Money? It was a constant problem—not to avoid clichés out of false modesty, a grip, a vise. But it was the last thing I could have mentioned to my mother; she would have thought right away that I was asking for a loan. Her eyes would fly up in startled alarm, fearful, barring the way.

Men? Even worse—unspeakable. You are aware that something is lacking, something is needful; you have to seek some remedy for your life and you call this stupor "love." That's the answer, it's simple—all you need is a man. ("A nice boy." "Serious.") But where are you to find this man? Who is he? What's in it for him, by the way?

And the facts of experience are far different.

I go to the office of a doctor who is treating me for an infection; when I'm ready for the examination, legs spread on the table, he suddenly goes down on me. I yelp, give a start—looking up I see his long bald head, speckled like an egg, grinning between my thighs. I think the brutality of this gesture was what finished me; too much craziness.

No, this is not the answer. But this is what I get. And I was sick to death of this predatory stuff, sick of being the unattached, available woman, walking around like a sort of sexual bomb. Besides, the truth is simple: this was not my need.

My mother couldn't bear to have thought that we—mother and daughter—were not absolutely devoted (though under present circumstances the facts could speak for themselves). A man I did not know very well had sent me a dozen long-stemmed American Beauty roses; my mother tried to pass them out to the nurses: "Take one! Take one!" she urged them gaily.

Several times a day a woman in a white jacket walked in the door, carrying a tray of dark-red tubes. Gravely, lips pursed, she would suck my blood through slim pipettes; it rose in thin red columns, in thick black gouts. My arms were covered with lush purple bruises, a result of all the needles. Once again my mother was concerned about the public opinion.

What would people think? What would people say? Luckily, till now I had been too sick to have any phone calls or visitors. People were asking about me. What could we tell them? And now there was talk of sending me to W-3— the psychiatric ward! What if *that* got out? Where were her friends to address their gifts and get-well cards *then*? (I didn't care about calls and cards, but they were her due: she ran her legs off going to bridal luncheons, wedding receptions, baby showers, buying cards and gifts for other people's children. It was her turn now.)

Why tell people anything? Why not tell them the truth? It seemed so much simpler.

"Ah, you don't care," she said, her dark eyes lowering reproachfully.

Right. I never cared what anyone thought, that was my trouble. I never took the consequences, I didn't have to face anybody. And my mother's whole life was facing people. It was the same old story—concealment.

All I knew was this: I couldn't take it anymore, no longer could bear this burden of concealment. Things seemed bad enough without adding extra weight. I wanted to be rid of it all, all of it. I wanted to abandon all this personal history—its darkness and secrecy, its private grievances, its well-licked sorrows and prides—to thrust it from me like a manhole cover. That's what I had wanted all along, that's what I was trying for when I swallowed those pills—what I hoped to obliterate. That was my real need. It had at last expressed itself, become all powerful.

"Tell people where I am," I whispered. "And ask them what they want me to make for them."

An idle boast. I never managed to finish any of my projects in occupational therapy—my baskets and key chains and beads. I was far more ready for W-3 than I thought.

II.

Iris had posted herself in the lounge with her cigarettes, emery boards, and stationery, writing letters on a silk-trousered knee. One hand fanned and fluttered the while, drying her nail polish. She was new to W-3; arrestingly tall, white faced, with frosted gray bangs and a black Nehru jacket buttoned to her chin. But her eyes were smeared; her pasted lashes sank like weights. In other words, like the rest of us, she seemed untidy. We were looking for such signs, of course: *What's wrong with her? Why is she here?* "Here" being the small psychiatric ward of the sprawling university hospital.

On the windowsill there would be some withered, dusty plant, long dead, still wrapped in bows and silver foil from the florist's: inmates received them rarely. Magazines accumulated all over the place, discarded heaps, old *Time*s and *Newsweek*s mostly; no one read them. The cupboard was crammed—boxes of puzzles, games protruding from every angle. All those boxes would have tumbled down at once if anyone ever attempted to disturb them. No one ever did.

The manifestation, therefore, of a stylish middle-aged woman in lounging pajamas, dashing off her correspondence and doing her nails, should have been tip-off enough; this was no place for such ordinary pursuits. But it seemed, after all, normal. Supremely.

Iris described herself as a "manic-depressive of twenty-seven years' standing." This, the first thing next morning at community rounds when, as a new patient, she was called upon to introduce herself to the group. For most, such a request could only come as a shock—at least it had for me. But in Iris I detected no hesitation and no irony either.

"Do I stand?" was all she asked.

No, she could sit. She straightened her shoulders, cleared her throat, and launched promptly and forcefully into an account of her life from age twenty-one—her first diagnosis. Her voice was strong, imposing, like her presence. She was counting on the platinum tips of her fingers. It was plain that she meant to begin at the beginning and to leave nothing out.

This was not the customary response. This was a power play. Iris was claiming seniority, like a bird in a barnyard. Too bad other patients—less seasoned—were too inexperienced to appreciate it. But it wasn't aimed at us, other inmates, anyway; this was directed at the doctors. Iris was not taken in by all this community stuff, the illusion—successfully maintained with a good many of us—that it was our relationship with other patients that was of importance to us, that was going to help us. She had been around long enough to know that her survival in a mental ward depended upon her status with the doctors. *They* were the ones who doled out the pills, the passes, and finally, the discharges. She knew the score and she was letting them know.

She was stately, strikingly erect. Her eyes were an indelible cosmic blue. She ticked off her fingers, arching them backward. Twenty-seven years to go! But we were glad to let her talk; it meant we wouldn't be called upon, wouldn't draw fire; we could be safe, we could be private, even, while Iris told us the story of her life.

We had many meetings. Patients' meeting—our own self-government with duly elected officials—two nights a week; team meeting, a smaller, more intimate group, one or two afternoons; and this one, community rounds, the first thing after breakfast every morning except Sunday.

Rounds—that's a hospital word, part of the doctors' daily routine, checking up on all their patients. But this occurs to me only just now—obviously I didn't figure these things out right away. You figured nothing out; you accepted. At first these words, names—everything seemed to be named—had a brash strangeness, the strangeness of the surroundings. The brashness perhaps in the mind, a bright, stunned state; everything rang out audaciously, like solid brass. If you have swallowed a lethal dose of sleeping pills, your experience moves from the plane of the particular to the general. I didn't understand this yet. Still, the surroundings were strange, all the same. Meetings? Why meetings? In this place?

This was the situation I had found myself in, my first morning on W-3; a newcomer, just delivered, sitting in the lounge and waiting for rounds to begin, clutching to my lap a little flat gray box of tissues—boxes distributed liberally all over the ward. Weeping was mightily encouraged here. I did not much feel like weeping, but wasn't so sure either that a sudden cloudburst might not overtake me. The prevailing winds being uncertain. I felt doubtful and uncertain about my appearance, too. My arms and legs were covered with sinister bruises and my hair had been clipped—shorn, skinned practically—like when I used to have lice as a child and got my head dunked in kerosene. I was wearing a short bunchy housecoat of faded terry cloth, and a pair of wide—gaping—pink slippers. They were several sizes too large to begin with and already well stretched with wear. Whose wear? I didn't know where these items had come from, but they were all I seemed to have; and I had been forewarned: on W-3 all inmates were expected to wear "clothes." This had me worried. But it meant, apparently, anything that was not hospital garb—no uniforms.

That did not make the disorderly assortment I saw around me any less drab. Patients in nightgowns, pajamas, robes, wigs, wraithlike in towels heavily draped over their heads, with sleepy, hanging faces, were finishing breakfast and reluctantly dragging chairs across the dining hall into the lounge. The plastic armchairs and sofas were already filling up; doctors were seating themselves, parting the tails of their long white coats. While we waited, I contemplated my feet resentfully in the loose pink slippers.

Perhaps once a month an inmate turned up with a voice like mine; invariably an attempted suicide who had spent several days in a coma in the intensive care unit before being transferred. Everyone knew what it meant. The coughing machine with its snorkels and seething mists rolled down the corridors, seeking me out. The coughing must have sounded like terminal agonies—like my voice. But inmates who had been around long enough recognized and accepted these peculiarities immediately. They nodded as soon as I opened my mouth: Zelma had had "that voice"; she had been trailed about by "that machine." Zelma had been released only a few days before I came—though she had promised to return. And now there was me.

I should explain right away that I didn't belong here. But that goes without saying, no one belonged here. That was the ordinary, the average, you might say the normal, reaction. On W-3 you encountered the terrible force of a generalization, and it had to be resisted, the self had to be exerted. Anything to deny this grim, inert, collective state.

The first thing I noticed was the uniformity of appearance, the carelessness of expression, dress. Everyone looked essentially the same—peculiar. Peculiar was what I expected everyone to be. So that seemed to be the explanation for these first impressions. I didn't understand that we were all in the same straitened circumstances. You don't get much notice for a trip to a place like W-3; there's no chance to pick and choose, to pack your bags and powder your nose. All of a sudden your number is called, you are claimed; you pick yourself up and come as you are.

There was another, more powerful, explanation for the general aspect of negligence—and that was the drugs. Drugs were far and away the most pervasive fact of life on W-3, but I didn't know that yet. I was not put on drugs automatically because of the medication I was still taking for my lungs. (I had a touch of pneumonia, not an uncommon occurrence here either.) So I was seeing them in action—a rare privilege, for a patient. But I could not account at first for the slurred voices, thick-tongued faces, the strange, uniform shrugging indifference. It horrified me. I thought it was the inmates themselves I was seeing, and that these people must be very different from me.

What if suicide is a sin? That is, to die benighted, in a state of total ignorance? If so, I had almost committed the sin, for I had come very close to dying—unhousel'd, unanointed, unanneal'd, no reckoning made but sent to my account with all my ignorance upon my head. That was the real truth of my condition, stripped to its essentials. I sat there, gripping my Kleenexes and gazing into my lap.

The room fell silent. Community rounds was about to begin. I looked up, ready and willing to pay attention; all this was new to me, and I was wondering what the meeting was going to be about. At once a freckled nurse with a blond ponytail and sweater sleeves knotted about her shoulders called upon me. *Would I introduce myself? Would I tell everyone what I was doing here?* This was a surprise! My neck was still craning with curiosity, but now, it seemed, I was to be the curiosity. Heads were turning, everyone was discovering me. The nurse, apparently presiding, was smiling at me encouragingly—indicating my whereabouts with an outstretched arm. She was doing this to make sure I knew who was meant: no one else was in doubt. All those other faces had turned on me like a shot. Raised without expression. Some fifty faces in a circle several rows deep. Some of these faces I had already encountered walking about the ward—fixtures of the place. So they had seemed. They now for the first time took on a dimension of recognition, familiarity.

An old fellow, a wizened black man with a fringed bald head, had swung his chair around and sat facing backward, looking away from the center of the room. I had noticed him earlier, at breakfast, smoking in the same way with his back to the table. "That's poor old Jesse." His long, powerful-looking arm moved across his chest, feeling in his shirt for matches; tufts of cotton stuck out of his ears. A small coppery-skinned black girl in a pink peignoir was curled up sleepily in an armchair, plucking large pink hair curlers from her head and dropping them into her lap. Deronda. I looked toward Deronda, hoping for a cue.

She yawned, cat's slits, behind a fist of Kleenex. She knew what it was like. I would have to find out for myself. These faces, waiting, conveyed no information: they didn't care one way or another whether I answered or not—just so long as, whatever I did, it took up enough time.

I didn't feel like telling this bunch of strangers how greedily I had wolfed down a whole bottle of sleeping pills; or about the considerable time I had spent in livid imagination, laying my cheek to the greasy doors of cold gas ovens. I didn't feel like telling them anything. I could explain, all right, but it would take too long. It would take my whole life. I could sense it behind me, cold, submerged, like an iceberg.

I declined to speak, on account of my voice.

"What's the matter with her voice? Can't she speak up?"

A pair of long blunt sideburns; a compact, forceful body in a white lab coat. This was Dr. Lipman, the head of the ward; most patients called him "Lipton."

"Is that why you're here? You can't talk? There's something

wrong with your voice?" Cigar smoke irritably surrounded him. He seemed to think this hoarseness was a symptom! But the voice was extremely characteristic; even other patients, in the midst of their own preoccupations, had grasped my situation without any difficulty. How come he, a doctor, didn't know?

It never occurred to me that this was a ploy. I had had no experience to speak of with the psychiatric sector before; and anyway I felt new—tender. I think I was expecting some sort of moratorium at first. For things to be more gradual, or some sort of exemption to be made in my case. But moratorium, armistice, truce, respite—that was what you never got on W-3. You plunged right in, in medias res, and life went on twenty-four hours a day. This was the hardest thing to get used to. Since this life was so plainly arbitrary and unreal, it often seemed to me that there would be no harm in it if every once in a while the pretenses were dropped, the flag was waved, the truce declared. But that never happened.

I tried to explain: there was nothing "wrong" with my voice, I just didn't have any.

"I can hear you," the freckled nurse insisted, ever prompt. Ever cheerful. This mode of pursuit was to become very familiar.

"Well I can't, dammit!" said Dr. Lipman, his starched coat scraping audibly as he shifted in his chair. His gruffness at least seemed more genuine; it really was impossible to hear me.

"Oh! I can hear her perfectly well! How about you people back there?" The blond ponytail spun about. "Back there," the rows of faces nodded. It didn't matter, they didn't need to listen. Forty-five minutes had to be used up, one way or another—that was all that mattered.

These are not impressions after the fact; then and there I grasped the essentials. It was early yet, no one else seemed moved to speak; I could not be let off so easily. Time was our common oppressor.

"Why don't you stand up?" the nurse suggested.

By this time I had already revealed anything anyone really needed to know about me. It never mattered what you said you were doing here. Some outward sign, some characteristic peculiarity, something all the rest could recognize right off—that's what mattered, that's what you were doing here. A certain point had been reached; no one had to hear how.

I must have seemed the only inquisitive person left in the room as I got—somewhat gropingly—to my feet, feeling for my Kleenexes, with my head poked to one side.

"There!" the nurse said. "Now everyone can hear you."

Hear me! Hear me! But the voice that was coming from me was not my own voice! How could they hear me?

Each of us had a story—as long, as involved, as hoary as Iris's—though few had the wind to launch into it. But Iris was overwhelming. After ten or fifteen minutes she was still strongly holding forth, her shoulders upright, her neck as stiff as ever in her black silk collar—still counting on her fingertips. And she hadn't used up the first hand yet!

I looked around the room. Guz had folded his arms—white to the elbows with tape—and gone back to sleep, his big, deep, trustful body collapsed in the chair. His feet were sticking out in bloody socks. Simone stuck her hands above her bowed head, catching up on her prayers. Her long black fingers rippled with bones. This was always unsettling. At such times it seemed to me that she was the only one who had any real grasp of our situation. But one thing was clear: Iris was crating no tension, no interaction. Our "community" was suffering a relapse.

Night and day we were a "community"; the fact was relentless. This Unit Is Not To Be Used As a Thoroughfare—the sign on the thick glass door spelled it out. Though the ward was locked, our doors must be at all times open. Patients must have roommates; except for those in isolation (and they were envied for it, and for their locked doors), we were not to be alone. The little rooms with their dormitory bunks, colored bedspreads, plastic desk lamps were not to be a refuge. We were expected to be out, out in the communal areas of the ward: in the rec room, lounge, occupational therapy; gathered round the piano or pool or Ping-Pong tables (the eternal triumvirate of psychiatric wards); active, participating, colliding with life—life that was to be found somewhere out there and not in ourselves. Demonstrably not. The faces at our meeting were lifeless enough. Faces: present and accounted for. We were faces, not bodies and souls.

Dr. Lipman interrupted Iris at last, pulling on his glowing cigar: "We'll get back to this next time." "Next time," Iris was put on lithium and fell silent. Disheveled bangs flopped on her brow—very distracting as she bent over her boxes of stationery, scribbling away. Her great smeared eyes were blank and cloudy, like cosmic dust.

We spent a lot of time grooming ourselves on W-3 and the results were always like this. The faces looked streaked, slept in; they lacked freshness and luster. There was inevitably something "wrong" about the hair. But much was made of it: street dress was the rule; shoes; inmates were not supposed to sit around in wrappers and slippers. Especially undesirable was the hospital issue—striped seersucker robes and outsize pajamas with loose tapes and strings. That was out. Two electric shavers were kept at the nurses' station—one was for legs. You might be sent from a meeting to put on lipstick or comb your hair. This because concern for one's appearance is commonly understood to be a criterion of mental health, one of the vital signs. The trouble was, most inmates were already concerned—passionately.

Most of us had arrived through the emergency room with

just the clothes on our backs—hatless, coatless, barefoot, in blankets. This matter of appearance was a constant distress. For almost everyone, for at least the first few days, this was the primary practical problem: How to get some things together. A toothbrush. A comb.

"Are you ready?"

That was the first thing I was asked. A bearded fellow in a white coat was peering at me through the bars of my bed. I was upstairs, in the room where I had been lectured by my private nurse Henrietta, and it was the first time the subject of W-3 was ever broached to me.

I was silent, considering. Actually I wasn't even thinking about the doctor's question—I was just waiting for a suitable interval to elapse before I made my reply. Ready for what? Who could answer such a question? I didn't know if I was ready; I didn't know what to expect from W-3 and I didn't know what to want from it, either. In fact I didn't want anything. I had been threatened with a jail sentence as the alternative. W-3 was the lesser of two evils (it usually was). Every one of us must have entered under more or less the same conditions.

But that wasn't what the doctor had meant.

"I mean do you have clothes to wear?" he went on. "You have to wear clothes, you know, on W-3."

So. Even the state of readiness, willingness, had something to do with clothes, with this matter of appearances. Inmates in fact were constantly talking about "getting some clothes"—our major concern. We were in one place, our belongings in another. It was not so easy to bring about a reunion.

Frankie was still wearing the shorts and sleeveless summer blouse she had had on when she was admitted—abruptly. It was now October. Also her shiny black wig, drawn down over her eyes, slanting and crooked like a roosting wing. She was subdued now, on lithium; I had missed the other, the dramatic, the dangerous Frankie—the one who had ripped out a toilet bowl with bare hands and threatened to kill every other female on the ward. ("Why don't you get your *own* man?" she'd said.) Too bad. It was plain that in those days other inmates had admired Frankie, envied the authenticity of her violence. Where did it go when she sat now—slack jawed, stoop shouldered, a heavy hump—sinking her ear over the phonograph in the rec room? You had to lean close; there was no amp. The sound came directly from the scratching needle, skipping and jumping in the old warped grooves: Bessie Smith, Billie Holiday, murmuring like mosquitoes. Everything on the ward had seen better days. The rec room was full of dusty, disabled equipment propped up in corners—looms, Exercycle machines. Everything was broken. The battered piano with bandaged keys and thudding pedals. The Ping-Pong table held together by matchbooks and splints.

Frankie hung her head, listening; it was just force of habit. Her lip stuck out, her eyelids drooped; the heavy whites glistened in her smooth black face.

Drugged to the eyes. That's what they say, and it's the truth. The drugs relax the facial muscles; the muscles cease to do their ordinary everyday work, keeping the chin up and the lip stiff. The lids droop; the cheeks hang; the mouth loosens. But all this is somehow fixed, stiff, another kind of mask; an immobility of expression.

Did you ask a question? The bucket is lowered, fetches up an answer.

But this was, more or less, the face of the ward.

Frankie's husband had locked her out in the hall: "Let the neighbors call the police." Now she had to find herself a job, an apartment—and her *own* man. (But this was characteristic. Our lives always seemed to be starting from scratch. It was as if you had to back yourself into a corner first; divest yourself of everything; cast off, cut adrift, abandon the world before you entered here.) What was holding all this up, what had kept Frankie immobilized, out of action so long, stuck in this place— was the fact, she said, that she had nothing to wear.

Almost daily she reported that her clothes were on the way. She described her wardrobe, the various outfits she had sent for, running her hands over her body, troubled by its bulges, sags, the tail of her blouse hanging out. She seemed worried that people wouldn't really believe her; and they didn't. You couldn't help wondering if these "clothes" that everyone seemed to be talking about all the time actually existed.

Trudy's clothes were locked in the trunk of a car belonging to a boy she had met the night before: Sleepy. She remembered his friends' names too: Happy, Dopey, Sneezy. They were helping her move. It was not clear where she was coming from, much less where she was going. She meant to stay in the car for a while. She had the clap. When she started acting funny, doubled up with cramps of peritonitis, hobbling about howling with her fists in her belly, the boys got scared, dressed her in someone's T-shirt and khakis, and delivered her to the glass doors of the emergency room—which opened, sweeping inward, sucked her in.

Sometime during the night Trudy was wheeled upstairs; admissions occurred at all dark hours on W-3. You always knew when someone had come; there was a great clatter of carts and heels and rousing voices—quarrelsome, distorted in the empty corridors. There was never an attempt to subdue any of it. For whose benefit? Our nights were more wakeful than our days. In the dark, when you could have used a little of the deathly calm that hung over those pale ocher walls in the middle of the afternoon, noisy life revived, came climbing out of the woodwork.

This time, however, the formalities of admission seemed needlessly prolonged and unrestrained. One voice especially, cackling and clamoring, sounded like a whooping crane.

Awakened thus, behind the bolted window gate (the key was like a tire iron), you could never make out what was being said—why the dam had burst. The words were always incomprehensible. You tried to gauge—from the decibels, the degree of the disturbance—how much excitement to expect. I was expecting a lot.

Each new arrival meant someone you were going to have to contend with, to live with—like living with your own conscience. But it was often days before the rest of us caught a glimpse of a new inmate in isolation.

The high windows of the isolation cells, three or four in a row, overlooked our exercise deck—a ruddy surface like a tennis court, surmounted by barbed wire and steep gray walls: limestone and gargoyles, the Gothic pinnacles of the great university. It was perfect autumn weather—warm, transparent, bright. You could have kissed the sky. It was so blue it tingled. But I never remembered what I was doing there until I saw the barbed wire springing up, flattening itself against the sky. It jolted me—as if I had touched it; as if something in me wanted to climb startlingly too.

Here Trudy seemed to be lying in wait, listening for the sound of footsteps passing under her window.

"Come and see me!" a voice called out as I was shuffling slowly past on the deck. It was a harsh, brash, demanding voice, flat, metallic, only you couldn't see who it might belong to through the barred window. I poked my face against the screen and peered into the scanty darkness.

"Who are you?" the hidden voice, unexpectedly close, demanded to know. I might have asked the same question. "I'm lonely!" (From the darkness.) "Come and see me!"

None of us was to remain in the dark about Trudy for long.

Through an administrative brainstorm, she had been placed in the cell with the broken toilet—Frankie's masterpiece. Frankie had been powerful in her fury; omnipotent, it seemed. There was a hole at the porcelain base you could put your foot through. I guess she had put her foot through it. Trudy was supposed to be in bed, being fed intravenously; it was thought she might have appendicitis—doctors have to hedge their bets. But she had no use for bedpans. She was lonely, naturally gregarious, like a penguin on some stony island; isolation was literally intolerable for her. Therefore she came into our rooms, seeking.

Seeking what? How should I know? How should she?

Trudy was charmingly pretty; a clear shining blond with remarkably white skin, sturdy, solid fleshed like a child. Her wrists and ankles had a touching thickness; she looked much younger than she really was. (Although that was nothing new; it was often hard to tell.) But Trudy instantly made a highly original and energetic impression: trudging along barefoot in flopping hospital pajamas, her short blond hair swinging at her cheeks—and pushing a tall creaking contraption. This was her intravenous stand—inverted bottles, tubes, and all. Everywhere that Trudy went, the stand was sure to go. It had to, she was attached to it; hooked up—one hand pinned and taped flat to a board. That didn't seem to deter her though.

"Knock knock," she'd say, announcing herself as she rolled up, shoving—hitching up her pajama bottoms with their loose tapes streaming. "Can I use your toilet, hey?"

We all knew about the gonorrhea.

"Can I use your telephone? Can I use your mirror?"

No telephones and no mirrors in isolation.

If you said no it was "Kiss off, fuck face"—without any malice—and she'd hitch up and move on to the next door. It never even occurred to you to wonder how she had managed to get out; she was obviously such a determined character.

I gave Trudy permission to use my makeup. She lugged her stand over to the sink and—one handed but expert—began to grind my dark powder, black pencil, red lipstick into her pure, blond features. She rubbed and patted and turned her cheeks this way and that in the lit tin mirror.

The smooth blond crown of her head was chattering away in the same brusque style.

"That's sure some weird sore throat you got. What'd you do? Cut it or something?" she asked me flatly, scouring her lips with the tube. She rubbed them together. "*Take pills!* Oh that's nothing, I do it all the time. I took a hundred seventeen aspirins once." Convinced she was reassuring me.

I was still walking around in my borrowed robe and slippers, with a cropped head and a croaking voice—another strange bird on the ward. One of those who had no place to live, nowhere to go. My flat had been vacated, the boxes I had packed were scattered now. My mother had brought my purse, which was why I had this junk, but nothing else seemed forthcoming.

It didn't surprise me in the least that Trudy wanted to fix her face up, make some effort on her own behalf—that was nothing special, that was just W-3. We all had to do the best we could. What did surprise me was how much. She just kept going, slapping it on, her little nose tilted. ("If I make the lips more scarlet... and the eyes more bright...") I watched with astonishment. The new face that was emerging—eyeing itself shrewdly—was clownish, whorish; heavy, dark, theatrical above the white throat. Her eyebrows were perfect black hemispheres. She stood on tiptoe, holding her pajamas up, looking for the face she had before the world was made. These were the facts that existed independently of the rules. Before the rules were made.

Guz was another who had nowhere to go. He had been evicted; his landlord had his clothes. His wife was divorcing him. Things were not going his way. He had slashed his wrists, knelt down to pray, thought better of it; crawled out into the hallway—bumping along on his knees and holding his arms up—coursing with blood. This was the way he was still holding them when he appeared among us: a huge strong-looking black with a thick neck and supple, shining skin; in a tattered undershirt and blood-spattered trousers soaked from the knee downward; in a daze. His arms extended, held up to view—sleeves of white tape. He seemed afraid to lower them or to let them touch his body; he couldn't quite get used to them yet, couldn't believe in the life that had almost departed through them.

I ran into this apparition in the hall—this large, dark, powerful, confused, blood-spattered creature—waving arms like bandaged stumps and swaying unsteadily on his feet. It was the first time I had seen him—like encountering a bear in a forest. We were not natural enemies, but my heart leaped. He mumbled something. I realized at last that he was asking me where he could find the clean laundry. But for days he walked about in his blood-soaked socks and shoes.

The same thread ran through most of the stories. The whereabouts of our clothes had something to do with the circumstances of our lives, our estrangements. We understood this instinctively; that's what had us so worried and confused. If we could just get body and soul together! *Why did the staff harp on that string?* Something was wrong, there was some discrepancy somewhere. So much easier to detect it in others. Frankie for instance: her black wig knocked over her eyes, a crooked lid—as if someone had jostled her with an elbow in passing. One glance at her and anyone would look round with wild surmise. Out there on the ward, the low afternoon sun swimming through the stripes of long barred windows like a goldfish in a gloomy tank, were all these apparent varieties of strangeness—as wrinkled, as demoralizing, as any hospital uniform.

Years before, in labor with my first child in a hospital in another large city, I was given scopolamine, twilight sleep. A drug I had asked not to be given. ("That's not scopolamine?" "No no, dearie, just something that will make you feel better.") With scopolamine you feel the pain, every bit of it, you yell your head off; you just don't remember it afterward. It knocks out the center of consciousness. At some point there was a lapse; I came to the surface. I was in some sort of large crib with bars pulled up on both sides, and a snugly masked nurse was leaning over me. I could see my big belly moving under contorted sheets. "Get your legs up there! You fat bitch, you! Move! Cow!" the nurse was saying through her mask. I was not offended. But why is she talking to me as if I can't hear her? I asked myself, and went out, as they say, like a light.

The next time I came to for an instant I was being given ether; I recognized the smell from a childhood tonsillectomy. *If it's ether I better breathe in.* I expanded and sank and went under again. But for days after I couldn't figure out why my throat was so sore.

There were many moments like this on W-3. The lucid bubble surfaced—then popped.

Everyone had to fill out a psychological questionnaire of some sort—five hundred closely printed queries. "I like tall women." "I hate my father." "I suffer from gas pains." "I believe in God." True or false? One must be pure in heart indeed to answer such questions. Some appeared more than once: Was this to trap you in deceit, or did it present a second chance at redemption? Or was it to confuse you, keep you guessing? The test was machine scored; you had to mark the answer between dots with soft pencil.

I still didn't know what had happened—what was happening—to me, and I couldn't understand why I was having such a hard time with this test. My head felt dull as soon as I bent over it; my hands shook; the brightness hurt my eyes; the white pages seemed to crackle, give off heat, about to burst into flame in my face. The dots were troublesome too—too small. I kept having to count the spaces over. I kept right on, pondering, trembling.

When I handed the test in later the same day, the nurses seemed taken aback. It occurred to me that I hadn't been expected to finish it right away—ever, maybe—and that my confusion was a more widespread, general condition. Maybe it had something to do with why I was here? It was a place where nothing was completed.

Finish what you're doing first was one of the nurses' favorite slogans.

After two months Simone had not finished this test. Passing her open doorway I could see her faithfully slaving away at her desk lamp, her head tucked in as if over her prayers. Her glasses, gropingly thick, almost dropped onto the paper. Her head seemed to fizz in the dull orange glow.

Most inmates didn't seem to feel as I did about the drugs, didn't dread them. I was not initiated. Medicines made the rounds at meals, dispensed at table in little paper cups. Every time Simone took her medicine—some clear viscous liquid, I don't know what it was—she'd topple off her chair and fall under the table in a sort of gurgling fit. Just like that. The response was automatic, instantaneous, it was almost one motion. She'd tilt her head back, the cup to her lips, you'd see her throat give a jump—and she'd slide right over like a camera shutter. You could hear the stuff bubbling. It sounded indignant. Her speech was the same way—rapid and sputtering. She always protested: I don't need any help! Her thin neck stretched out, her glasses thick as the bottoms of Coca-Cola bottles, she'd right herself, climbing to her knees. The whole performance struck me as spectacularly repulsive. I never got used to it. But as time went on, I understood it was the drugs.

Simone, in fact, was very fastidious about her person, although that was not the first thing that would occur to you when you saw her groveling under the table. She washed her garments from the skin out every night and straightened her hair with an electric iron in the kitchen, brandishing the rod like a red-hot poker; smoking and sizzling with boar tufts of singed hair.

Hair was always a problem, but for the black women it was a scourge. They couldn't cope with it. Wigs and towels were standard items on W-3; most women, black or white, wrapped their heads up in towels, attempting to hide or "control" their hair. Even the cleaning women wore wigs. Our corridors seemed always in the process of being scrubbed by thin-legged black women in dark-blue uniforms, thrusting their mops with a strange listlessness, biting their cigarettes. They came from the same ghettos surrounding the hospital. Evidently it took some effrontery, in that society, to present oneself without such a smooth shiny wig. It took too much. So the struggle continued: there was no letup here, no mercy. By night the kitchen reeked of strong burning hair.

Simone's "clothes" were in the house of her sister who had her committed, who was now her greatest enemy in the world. She wouldn't set foot in that house again for anything— anything, that is, except her clothes. After all this time, she was still scheming to get hold of them. At patients' meeting, when we took up passes and privileges, Simone always had the same request—her one and only request. Unless she was rocking back and forth, wrathfully muttering her prayers to herself, in which case you couldn't interrupt her. She prayed with sinister effect for our souls.

What Simone wanted was for a nurse to accompany her in a taxicab to her sister's house. She told us her plan: The nurse was to distract the sister while Simone sneaked in and rounded up all the things she needed—she knew exactly where they were. If she could only lay her hands on them! Then Simone and the nurse would make their getaway in the taxi—while the sister, discovering too late what they were up to, would run out just in time to see them making off with their bundles and would be left standing on the doorstep shaking her fist.

By now Simone, beside herself, carried away by her description of this imaginary scene, would spring up, her voice chokingly thick, and begin throttling her fist. Like the black power salute.

After I had heard this request a few times I began to see why Simone emphasized the nurse so much. She was not asking for a pass for herself, any personal liberty—she wanted to make that clear. She didn't mean to overstep any boundaries. The pass—freedom—was only for her "clothes."

One evening toward the end of dinner (I was still poking over my tray at the end of our two long tables, set at right angles like the corridors) a tall young woman came abruptly striding through the dining hall. She was all in black, evening dress, with bony naked shoulders and one long black opera glove all the way up to her armpit. The other glove struck out from her fist. An elongated face, raddled with rouge, black streaks drawn over her eyelids like wilted butterfly wings, and a coarse straw-colored wig, stiff and wadded; it looked like a nest.

The young woman was Zelma—a repeat performance. She marched in as if she owned the place. As if she had a pair of hounds tugging at a leash. Her long jaw thrust itself forward: BAM! BAM! it jolted with each stride.

There followed a heavyset fellow in a leather jacket, lugging suitcases; he had one in each hand, one under each arm. A cabdriver. The seat of his pants was baggy and broad, and he could barely pick his feet up. Behind him an attendant, equally burdened and creaking, scraped along, hauling a utilities cart. The last time, Zelma had arrived like me—rolled up in a blanket. This time she had come better prepared. Seven pieces of matched luggage, smooth pale leather; two wigs with stands; a portable TV (later to cause such a stir in the small affairs of the ward); a portable typewriter, and half a dozen stiff textbooks—medical tomes. Zelma traveled with her own pharmacopoeias.

All this was duly deposited inside the bright glass cubicle of the nurses' station. The attendant knelt down at once and started snapping open suitcases, looking for things that were not permitted on the ward: Pills, razors, scissors, knives—the lurid possibilities were endless. But especially pills. And especially with Zelma. She stood over him, cursing him out in a harsh, cracked voice—it was like a bark—and swatting him on the back with her long black glove.

Most of our attendants were grad students in the divinity school, big muscular clean-living types, all-American guys; ex-lifeguards and so on. His hands groped about the suitcases, felt the satin bindings; his football shoulders registered nothing. Naturally not. We, the inmates, were supposed to react with one another; our emotions were there to be aroused, our patience tried, our passions stirred; but the staff must not be moved. Nothing shocked, nothing provoked the staff. That was the rule.

According to the staff, there were "no rules" on W-3, and they would make "no rules." But of course there were rules, there were plenty of rules, there was nothing but rules—the air was thick with them. It was just that they were unsuccessful, like this one. The attendant didn't find anything.

Meantime the cabbie stood about with his hands in his pockets, a cigarette behind each ear, waiting to collect his fare.

Next morning at rounds Zelma protested first thing, in her distinctive, scraping voice: she didn't want a roommate; she demanded a room of her own. Morning haggard in her dressing gown, her brass hair (her own) full of greenish chemical highlights, the dirty black wings still drawn over her eyes. Her face reminded me of the "breadlines" standing outside the nurses' station every night when they dispensed the sleeping pills.

But it was plain that Zelma hadn't slept; I could imagine her eyes penetrating the darkness as they now penetrated our midst.

I don't know when it finally dawned on me that there was something the matter with Zelma's voice, like my voice, and for the same reason: voices from the tomb. You could still hear the characteristic hoarseness and croaking. But the loud abrasive voice seemed peculiar to her, to belong to her personality. As if she wore a studded dog collar round her throat.

"It's not that I have anything against a roommate!" she cried, looking all about. "I don't have anything against anyone! It's just that I have too much clothes with me. What would I do with all of it, where would I put it? It would take up too much room!"

Too much! This was a switch. But not really. All these suitcases were no exception to the rule. Zelma had been discharged just a short time before—and she had said she'd be back. Now here she was. So it seemed as if she'd merely been out on a pass, gone home to fetch her clothes. And this was the constant daydream of life on the ward.

III.

Prematurely Trudy appeared among us. She was supposed to be in isolation, still in bed, trickling into chilly bedpans; but she was a poacher by nature, like a cuckoo—she came and squatted on our toilets. It may be that the bottles and tubes were meant in part to restrain her; if so, it proved an idle hope. She perambulated down the corridors lashed to her intravenous stand—bandages, pajama strings loosened and streaming— looking like a sort of injured parade float. It was no use trying to keep Trudy hidden away (though that would be tried again, later on); all measures had failed, she was abroad anyhow. So the bottles and stand disappeared, and Trudy was allowed at last to come to the table. The stops were out.

Our trays came up a few at a time on the service carts; you had to look for the one with your name on it. But there was no tray for Trudy. She kept getting up and looking. She had borrowed a wrapper of thin blue cotton, sheer as a curtain, and she paced up and down, very determined, the short skirts whipping about her bare legs. Every time someone else approached the table carrying a tray, Trudy had to hike over to inspect it in case there had been some mistake. Her eyebrows vigorously blackened; her blond hair swinging at her cheeks. She was sticking her nose into all our trays, looking for her name.

Some of us were touchier than others. Davy Jones was tucking his napkin round his chin. He was a short, solid, husky young man; broad jaw, welded, all of a piece. Even on W-3, his shirt collars were stiff and his pants were creased; his mother and sister looked after his clothes, trotting back and forth with plastic bags and coat hangers.

"Take it easy," I warned Trudy in my hoarse whisper. Her blond hair was dipping into his tray.

Without turning round or raising his head—the back of his neck as thick and sunburned as a brick—Davy brought his buckled shoe down on her bare foot. He ground his heel.

Trudy squawked and gave a hop, clutching her toes.

"Never mind, it's all right," she told me, limping up, groping her way along the backs of the chairs, "I've been in nuthouses before."

At last a pot of tea and a dish of Jell-O were produced from the kitchen.

"Tea and Jell-O? This stuff sucks. I'm starving. They didn't let me eat anything for two days."

"That's why you have to eat lightly," Blanche told her primly.

"Hear that?" Trudy seized Blanche by the arm. "My stomach's growling. Listen to it! Listen!" she insisted, gripping and prodding the undernourished bone. Blanche, with her mouthful of tinny braces, was as thin, as pale, as lacking in vitality as any of the patients.

Trudy cocked her head and listened herself for a moment.

"It's not my fault. They made the mistake. They thought I had appendicitis. I didn't have appendicitis, I have gonorrhea. Look everybody! Look!" she cried, hiking up her skirts and climbing onto the table.

Knives, forks, tin covers scraped the trays in silence.

Trudy turned around, pulled down her pants, and stuck out her behind—presenting a pair of small tight buttocks. They seemed gripped, like fists. You could see the puncture marks, ringed with bruises, caked with blood.

"They've been shooting me full of penicillin," she confided, looking over her shoulder and hoisting her skirts still higher. "That just goes to show you it's the clap!"

"Put your skirt down, pull your pants up, get off that table, Trudy." Blanche sounded almost scandalized. Almost, because, by definition, she could have no such reaction. Her name tag, RN, was clipped to the pocket of her Girl Scout blouse. "Sit down and eat, your dinner's getting cold," she added, with more customary primness, spreading her napkin in her lap.

And yet it had seemed such an innocent demonstration. Like those old billboard ads of a child's backside and a potty. Try a little tenderness.

"Call this dinner?" Trudy sneered, climbing down and dropping her elbows on the table. She looked at her tray and leaned her knuckles against her lip. "There's no law says you can't eat just because you have the clap, is there?"

Her eyes, narrowed amid streaks of war paint, gazed round her greedily. Our silent meal persisted.

We mostly ate in silence. Over the two long tables the heads were bent, the eyes were lowered; only the forks and spoons were lifted. Barely.

Above our heads, a sign scribbled in crayon nervously predicted our forthcoming Halloween party. "Music! Games! Refreshments! Fun!" The letters trembled. It wobbled with exclamation marks. You could see at a glance it was the work of an inmate; some shaky hand.

The sign was already up there when I came; it smote me the very first time I ever set foot on W-3. It had been the middle of the afternoon, and for some reason the place was deserted; the bunks with their blue bedspreads, glimpsed through half-open doorways; the lounge with its dusty plants, discarded magazines.

The chairs were upended on the long dining tables. The floors were still damp and slick from their latest drubbing; buckets of foamy gray wash water stood about the hall. The nurse, my escort, was tiptoeing gingerly ahead of me over the wet floors, carrying my roses in a dripping glass jar. She wore flesh-colored stockings, low-heeled pumps, a navy dress with a Peter Pan collar. Nurses were required to wear street dress too—though this was so plainly a uniform. And it seemed to me that she was stepping so softly, sanctimoniously, in order to preserve a certain mood.

It was the mood of a childhood convalescence, of lying in bed with a blanket round my chin, a washrag on my brow, listening to the sounds of my mother going about her housework while she listened one after another to the daytime serials on the radio. Their sentimental sign-off music. As a matter of fact, someone—unseen—was actually playing the piano at that very moment. Hearts and flowers. Melodramatic. I didn't know what I had been expecting, but it all seemed pretty anticlimactic now.

Then the sign had caught my eye and my heart dropped like an anchor. A Halloween party. A gruesome thought. Was this what they wanted to do with me? I didn't want to be rehabilitated. It was not my deepest need. What was I doing here? What was I letting myself in for? What hole in the earth had I fallen into?

It was early October; the sky was snappingly blue, flagging away up there in the breach between stone walls.

· "Never mind," I said to myself, looking up at the sign. "It doesn't matter. I'll be out of here by that time."

And that was what I still told myself every time I raised my eyes to the wall.

Maurice got up to fetch a straw. He was a thin old man in a wrinkled pajama shirt. His footsteps in his loose carpet slippers fell with a dreadful, dragging regularity. I couldn't bear the sound of those shuffling feet, heard night and day.

The trouble was he trembled; trembled so badly he couldn't drink his soup—the liquid splashed in his spoon. He'd steady his elbows on the table, lifting the spoon, stretching forth his head on his gullied neck, puckering his long lips to meet it. And then the leap. You could have measured it on a seismograph. The soup splattered. He'd drop the spoon and sit back at once, wiping off his shirtfront with his thumbs.

At this point I would realize that there was a body inside this wrinkled shirt, and inside the body was a man. And there was not necessarily much connection between them. It was just that every time Maurice ducked his head over his soupspoon, someone, something, jostled his arm. And if he reached for his coffee cup, it started rattling against the saucer and chattering like teeth.

Maurice was a professor at the university (the stone walls of the great gray campus), an alcoholic (though that was never mentioned); the soul of politeness. He was treated with deference. On the night he arrived, for instance, I was sent into his room to say hello to him. There was a crowd round his bed, his thin bare yellow legs laid out in their carpet slippers. His gaunt profile, wrinkles dragging, stared up at the ceiling. I had the impression of approaching a bier. He talked without looking at anyone, without lifting or turning his head. But very courteously, persistently—the way he kept after his food.

For God's sakes, this was no time for courtesy!

Now Maurice pulled out his chair and sat down again. He stuck the straw into his soup bowl and leaned over, sucking, his eyes squeezed shut. They disappeared altogether in the thick yellow folds of his skin.

Trudy was eyeing my tray. "What's that?" she asked, pointing at a saucer. "It looks like shit."

"It does, doesn't it? But I think it's custard."

"Let me taste it." She dipped her finger in.

She got up and began to prowl up and down, up and down, scavenging for food between the two long tables. Her fists doubled in her pockets, her hair swinging like a bell. What's that? You gonna eat it? Don't be so stingy, shithead. Can I borrow your butter? Will you loan me your bread?—Why not? She had borrowed just about everything else. She had nothing of her own but a pair of panties, and those soiled and bloodstained, not even a tray with her own name on it, like everyone else. So now she was borrowing the food off our trays.

Gerda kicked out her chair. Finished. She always got up abruptly like that, with a thrust of her shoulders, a jerk like a gibbet—as if she meant to fling herself away. Sandy head, skin and bones, eyes downcast. It was the one decisive gesture she seemed capable of. But in the midst of this motion her force was already spent; her face was feebly expressionless. Her fingers— poking out of the thick gauze cast on her arm—were creeping after her cigarettes.

This arrested Trudy's attention. "Where's she going?" she wanted to know. "Is she coming back?" Addressing as usual the room at large and narrowing her eyes shrewdly as she licked a sticky thumb.

As a matter of fact there *was* something arresting about Gerda. Total negation. She drifted past. Absent. AWOL.

Gerda's room was at the near end of the corridor, closest to the nurses' station—the only room with regulation hospital beds, unlike all the other army-style bunks on the ward. You could see into its darkness from the tables; I watched her retreating into the remote white bed, the metal bars raised and gleaming.

It was the tray Trudy had her eye on. Naturally Gerda only picked at her food.

"Hey you!" Trudy called down the table. "Hey you! Excuse me for saying Hey you, I don't know your name. Hey you, gimme that tray. Pass it on here. I'll finish it!"

After dinner, patients' meeting. Patients presided. Trudy had not been to one before.

Sydney, our chairman, called the meeting to order, conscientiously cracking his knuckles. He was new to the job. A slight blond, built like a jockey. Black jeans; a greasy DA; a ruddy face, lumpy and purplish with acne. Now it had a pink, smug expression; I was told that, contrary to custom, he had wanted this office very much.

"Will the recording secretary please read the minutes of the last meeting?"

Trudy bounced up. "Who's got a cigarette? I need a cigarette. Someone gimme a cigarette." She stalked up and down in the midst of the chairs, calling out her steel-string voice.

These patients' meetings after dinner were sparsely populated. Gone were the stiff white coats that strode in and out so rapidly during the day. Now there would be only the nurses, at most two or three (there was a constant reduction in numbers, a sense of attrition as the day wore on, shrank toward night), sitting about like peaceful chaperones, their heads bowed over the hooked rugs in their laps. Hooking rugs was all the rage on the ward, though it was mostly the nurses who had such projects; they spent more time in occupational therapy than we did.

The cigarette lit, Trudy sat down, crossing her legs and flicking her skirt over her knees.

Fran began to read the minutes very loud and fast, holding the notebook up so I could see her black eyes moving. She wore a shower cap over her curlers; coarsely graying hair.

"What's she doing that for?" Trudy asked, puffing away.

"Shh. It's a meeting."

"Well I got a question. Can't you ask questions at meetings?"

"All right, what's your question?"

"What's she doing that for?"

Fran looked up. "Any additions or corrections?" she asked in a challenging voice. She seemed to be taking all this personally.

"Actually, I think I'm supposed to say that," Sydney said, glancing down at the notes of parliamentary procedure he was crushing in his fist.

Trudy was up. "I need an ashtray. Someone gimme an ashtray."

"Hey, Trudy. Cut it out. You're interrupting the meeting."

"Never mind, it's all right. You can wait a minute. Everyone else has an ashtray."

There were ashtrays all over the place full of stubbed-out cigarettes. Someone gave up theirs. Trudy sat down, skirt open, perching the ashtray on her bare knee. Daintily she tapped the ash from her cigarette.

"Then… the minutes… stand… as read…" Fran announced, very emphatic.

No one ever corrected the minutes. No one ever paid enough attention. Besides, patients' meetings didn't have to last, like all our other meetings. There was no specified time, no preordained duration. No need to drag out the proceedings interminably. The mood was impatient; most of us were anxious to get to passes and privileges, the main attraction.

"Any old business from the last meeting?"

Someone brought up some old business. Doris, of course, no one else would do such a thing. A dark, solid-fleshed housewife in her forties, with heavy folded arms and bright glossy eyes. There were groans of protest. But Doris smiled complacently; she knew what she was doing. It wasn't for our benefit.

Trudy interrupted again. "Hey! I got another question! When do *I* get to talk?"

"So far," Sydney observed, "you've been doing more talking than anybody else."

"Oh fuck. Fuck you. I know all about these meetings. Don't worry, I been to plenty of meetings. I bet I been in more nuthouses than you have. So you don't have to go getting stuck up with me about your dumb meeting! I know what goes on. They're all the same. A lot of yak-yak."

"Okay," Sydney said. "You get your turn to yak-yak when we come to passes and privileges. Everyone gets a turn then. Is that all right with you?"

Trudy liked that. She laughed appreciatively—a low-pitched giggle, a sort of murky gargle, way down deep in the back of her throat. We were all to become very familiar with this giggle.

I was impressed with the way Sydney had taken over the meeting, nervous as he was, glancing hastily at his notes and cracking his big knuckles. He was our best pool player, really marvelous; what a bridge he could make with his double-jointed thumb. I loved to watch him straddling the table, cocky, the size of a twelve-year-old, tossing back a hank of greasy hair and screwing up his eye. Twitching his pink nose like a rabbit. His eyes were watery, looked itchy and allergic. He knocked about the ward in his saddle-stitched jeans and elevator shoes, feeding coins to the Coke machine. The carbonation was poison to his kidneys (a congenital birth defect), the sweet syrup was obviously activating his acne; he smoked to the nub, to his bitten nails, the cigarettes that he was convinced were stunting his growth. But I found myself admiring him more and more.

We took up the question of passes and privileges. This was what everybody was waiting for. Privileges meant permission to leave the ward but not the hospital—to go to the canteen in the basement, for instance, or to the gift shop. You also needed privileges to go out onto the exercise deck without a nurse. Passes meant permission to leave the hospital itself, but only during the day, and you had to remain within the boundaries of the campus. For this you had to sign out. These rights were granted in perpetuity; you could use them at will. But if you were going beyond the boundaries, or staying out after dark, then you had to make a special, separate request. A weekend pass—but few of us requested weekend passes. Usually, only those who could not conceivably get one, like Flora, who in a few minutes was due to start whining in her soft Virginia drawl: "I want to go home. I don't like it here. When will they let me go home?"

Clutching her Kleenex and cigarettes, her head like a bag of red curls trembling on the sofa next to Fran's shoulder. Fran and Flora were roommates. Evidently it was hoped that Fran would be a good influence on Flora; inmates were often linked in this way. Maybe Flora would turn out to be as aggressive as Fran? Maybe her case would take the same bold revolutionary course? Anyway, Flora had already been elected (over the customary tearful protest) our next recording secretary.

Sydney called on Zelma.

Zelma was wearing her silver lamé mini, matching stretch boots; her thighs clutched close in silver-speckled tights. White lipstick. Zelma really did own a pair of white Russian hounds; they must have looked markedly like her, with their long pale faces, drooping ears, black-ringed eyes. She had been given a room to herself, and it was true: her things really did take up both tin lockers, both desks and chairs, both beds. One was piled high with discarded garments: belts, stockings, high-heeled shoes, delicate silk dresses with labels like Pucci, Carducci, Mollie Parnis. She stripped them off like banana skins. It was a high-class mess. Perfume bottles, lovely lotions, aerosol cans, hair curlers and skewers and bald-headed wig stands. Wadded Kleenexes, bits of paper—important personal messages. Zelma was always getting telephone calls. She was not one to mingle with our life. She skipped breakfast and lunch and occupied her chair at the dinner table as briefly as possible. But if the telephone began to ring somewhere down the corridors, she would abandon her knife and fork with a clatter:

"It must be for me. For me!" she'd call out, jumping up and stomping off with her slender jolting stride. And it usually would be too. Most of us never even looked up when the telephone started to ring—we weren't expecting any calls.

"I take that back," Trudy interrupted to deliver a sudden thought. "These places aren't really the same. It was much worse at Tyndall. All they do there is strap you down on a table and shoot you full of Thorazine. Wham. Both cheeks."

"Thank you for the tribute," said Sydney. "But you're out of order again. If you interrupt any more, I'll have to declare you out of order."

"*Big* deal."

"I want to go home."

"Hey, you're out of order," Trudy said.

"When will they let me go home?"

Answer: When you quit asking, dummy.

"Hey. Declare her out of order, declare her out of order."

"Sit down, Trudy."

"How come she gets to be out of order and I don't? How come you don't tell her to shut up like you're always telling me? I'm saner than she is anyway. It's not that I don't like you," Trudy added hastily, turning a serious face to Flora, afraid she was hurting her feelings. "I don't even know you. But you don't look so hot to me."

Flora rocked back and forth, whining and clutching her knees.

Trudy got up. "Someone gimme a cigarette. I need a cigarette."

"I just gave you one."

"I nigger lipped it."

"Too bad."

"You know what you can do."

"Look, Trudy. Keep it up and you go back to your room," Lucy said, intruding at last, her thumb in her blunt-tipped kindergarten shears.

"I don't want to go back. I can't even flush the toilet. Some loony made a hole in the john. Come see for yourself if you don't believe me."

"It's all right, we believe you," Sydney said. "We know all about your toilet. But you're out of order again."

"No shit, Sherlock."

"I want to go home. Go. Home."

Gerda got up with a jolt of her shoulders; she needed a light. She was a chain smoker and it was a familiar gesture; she was not allowed to have matches or to light her own cigarettes. She had changed her clothes since dinner; she changed repeatedly throughout the day. She put things on, thrust them from her with the same callous, sinister indifference; hung clothes on her body as she might toss them over a bedpost. Now it was a belted hospital robe. Her pale face swayed; the unlit cigarette dangled from her lips.

"How come she gets to get up for a cigarette and I don't?" Trudy complained. "It's not fair. What kind of joint is this! How come no one else is ever out of order around this place except *me*?"

"Either sit down now and shut up, Trudy, or leave."

"Okay kiddo. You said it. I'm leaving." Stomping out, fists doubled at her sides, the housecoat flapping open—flaunting naked thighs.

She glanced over her shoulder.

"Anyhow this meeting sucks," she said.

No one had wanted Trudy to leave. For the staff it was a failure, the cardinal sin. For the inmates it was also a failure. I couldn't help seeing our meeting now through Trudy's eyes.

We resumed our discussion of passes and privileges. All our requests were as familiar, as punctually predictable, as Flora's.

Zelma wanted a pass so she could go to a movie. That's what she always asked for, and it was always the same movie— *Titicut Follies*, a documentary about a state mental institution. Gritty shaved heads, naked bodies cowering in cold showers, that sort of thing. Life on W-3 wasn't brutal enough for her.

"You're welcome to come," she barked. "Really. All of you, any of you."

She always said that too. The doctors had let it be known that Zelma wasn't getting any of these passes until she exhibited more community spirit. But what was that supposed to mean? It meant, apparently, all these drab faces sitting around in a circle; everyone had to be included in everything. She looked around. I wondered if she was picturing what it would be like if all of us actually did accompany her, did follow wherever she went. A haunting spectacle. Like the livid, bedraggled queues shuffling up for their sleeping rations. No wonder she couldn't work up much enthusiasm.

"Come if you like. It makes no difference to me."

There was no irony at any of these meetings. All those textbooks in Zelma's room (if you could find them under the wigs, pins, powder) were psychology; she was immersed in the subject. She couldn't go to this movie about a mental institution because she herself was confined in a mental institution. But that didn't seem to impress her. No one took notice; it didn't appear in any way striking or remarkable. I couldn't blame her either. Life on W-3 did not have much reality for any of us.

We voted half-heartedly: Yes.

Jeffrey? This at least would be more interesting. He was one of our teenagers, president of his high school class, one of the highest-rated schools in the suburbs. On visitors' night the ward swarmed with his friends: bright, good-looking boys and

girls, fortunate youths; their buoyant faces were a contrast to the
faces of the ward. But none of them was so poised, so gracefully
lean, so purely, arrestingly attractive as Jeffrey—whom we had
in our midst. And yet he'd done time at Tyndall, like Trudy.

He slouched in his chair without self-consciousness, his
long legs sticking out in skinny stovepipe jeans, tapping his
bongo drums on his lap. The striking black forelock grazing
his eyes. He was sure to ask for a pass to attend some school
activity; a sorority dance, a cookout, a football game. What
was it this time?

"Donkey basketball. You play it riding on donkeys' backs."
Real donkeys? No kidding! Where?

"Where else? Where do they have basketball courts? Where
do they have nets? The gym!" Afterward there would be a dance,
a cookout on the beach, a swim….

"Oh boy, that's great, Jeffrey. That sounds terrific!" Sydney
had hoisted his arm up so high he seemed to be dangling from
it. "All in favor?" he demanded, his pink mug looking round
under his arm for other hands. They didn't fail to shoot up. No
need to count them this time! How we loved Jeffrey's plans,
only half-believing in them.

But as passes and privileges got underway, the mood
changed again, became more passive, resigned. No one was
really listening to anyone else. Each inmate was thinking only
of his own turn that was coming, counting round the circle of
faces to see how long it was going to take. Each was brooding
over his own special request.

When I was three years old, I was a flower girl at a wedding.
I wore ribbons in my hair, a formal of stiff peach-colored net,
and carried a cone-shaped bouquet of rose petals and paper
doilies. The flower girls—there were two of us—were supposed
to march primly down the aisle, smirking and nodding and

turning our heads from one side to the other, sprinkling rose petals as we went. We had practiced all this at rehearsal. Now the music was playing, the rows of chairs were filled, the white sheet was unrolled in our path. My comrade was an older, bigger child (about five?), with a headful of energetic-looking black curls and a large, aggressive brown mole on her cheek. What we called a birthmark.

We marched slowly, turning our heads from right to left, and all the faces turned and looked at us. All of a sudden the other little girl tucked her bouquet under her arm, gathered up her skirts—she was wearing long ruffled bloomers like a Southern belle—and made a run for it. I saw her heels trotting, the black curls bouncing on her head, as she raced up the aisle.

Hmm. I wonder if I'm supposed to do that?

The thought flashed through my mind. It was a novelty. The other girl was bigger than me; and she had looked mighty sure of herself, with the mole on her cheek, her satin bows all in motion as she bolted and ran. Maybe she knew something I didn't know. I had a strong urge to take off too. But I pressed slowly on, smiling from side to side and pinching the rose petals.

Every time I observed some outburst, some dissident behavior on the ward, I would feel the same urge, the same strong temptation. And the same thought would pop into my head, with the force of novelty—the way ideas occur to a child's mind:

Hmm. Maybe I should try that too?

I would want to break and run. I would want to shout and swear. I wanted to get up and stalk out of the meeting too. Maybe that was the thing to do. Some explosion was necessary. You never knew what blastoff, liftoff, might be the one. Even the staff recognized this—within limits. Inmates were drugged to the point of stupidity, then patted on the shoulder and urged to get it all out. Doctors thumped on the powder kegs and told them to cough.

Only one thing restrained me. If I also got up and ran out of the meeting, it would only be an imitation of Trudy. That was the trouble. There was no novelty. One gesture was stale, powerless, and unoriginal as the next. Nothing was original on W-3. That was its truth and beauty.

Gerda wants to go off the ward by herself; she wants to be alone. Gazing down at the muff of cotton wadding on her arm, her eyes heavy lidded—she doesn't try to lift them. The small dark sickle-shaped mouth opens and closes almost inaudibly.

Even so, you get the drift, the portent; it has been established that this is the one thing Gerda cannot do.

"I don't think Gerda is ready to go off the ward by herself," Lucy says, folding her rug and laying it aside—taking up the persevering tone that is always used on such occasions. "I don't think Gerda cares very much about herself. She's still burning herself with cigarettes."

There is a rumor on the ward that this sort of frankness is the way to salvation. A shortcut. Tears, incriminations, any sort of confession, exposure, self-betrayal will do. The gray boxes stand at the ready. But no reaction from Gerda. The lids of her eyes don't even flicker. This is no way to reach her. After all, she's an expert at immolation; she specializes in mortification of the flesh.

Gerda's seizures had begun quite recently, one day out of the blue while she was shopping in a department store. Or, what it came down to for her: the collapsing stair treads at the bottom of the escalator. She couldn't tell whether they were going up or down. And what were all those people staring for? I knew what it felt like to look at her, exposed, her thin legs spread out, urine escaping all at once like heat leaving the body. What did it matter what the strangers saw?

She'd had another seizure, fell and hit her head on the

radiator while smoking pot with Zelma and Davy in the kitchen. So now there's a soiled patch of bandage on the back of her head; she smokes, eyes downcast, ignoring it.

We vote yes nonetheless. We always vote yes. Sydney is counting the hands, muttering under his breath. But Gerda isn't paying attention anymore. She doesn't even seem to be listening. What does it matter what the strangers see?

Ah, Doris at last. She sits up willingly, tugging at the hem of her skirt as she shifts her weight in her chair. It so happens that Lucy is also tugging at her skirt, pulling it over her knees—whitened as knuckles in their taut nylons. They are both large dark women, perched in the same way.

This is going to be some small particular request: a trip to the canteen to buy two packs of Pall Malls; to the lobby for postage stamps. Made always with a sly mocking smile. Doris folds her hands on her knees.

She would like to mail a letter.

"Why don't you ask for a pass, Doris? You could get one," Sydney tells her encouragingly. "Don't you think it's time you asked for a pass?"

Doris shakes her head no, smiling at her lap. Her dark hair is combed, she wears bright lipstick; there is nothing disturbing about her appearance. In fact, the only thing discernibly wrong about Doris is this sly, safe way of hers—playing the game. On the ward we were under pressure to please; everyone understood this, it was basic. If you didn't please, you didn't get out. But you understood also that it was a deadly temptation, had to be resisted. This was what made Doris, with her dark, glossy eyes, something of a pariah. She seemed to be mocking our schemes with her modest requests. As she seemed to be mocking Lucy, with her schoolmarmish ways, compressing her lips and folding her hands.

All in favor?

And so on. Each request duly discussed, then voted on with a show of hands. Yes! Yes! Yes! But it makes no difference if we always vote yes. This is a mock tribunal. We have no power to grant passes—only to ask, like Flora. So what are we doing then? Why are we sitting here? Making our requests, voting? We are behaving—like Doris—mocking ourselves, playing the game.

Trudy was right. This meeting sucks.

I was anxious for my mother to go back to Florida as quickly as possible and take my sons with her. I saw this as their refuge. Sun, sea, clean air, and above all my father's protection. Whatever else he was—moody, bitter, blackhearted, as if he had the goods on life—a powerful man.

My father could fall asleep at the drop of a hat. Once he had been awakened by a cop—opening his eyes, he glimpsed the stomach, brass buttons—shaking him by the shoulder and announcing in a loud voice: "He's not dead." But it was no joke. He worked the night shift; to me he usually seemed to be sleeping. All day long we had to whisper and go on tiptoe while he lay snoring on his back—from time to time emitting sounds of a struggle. Even as a child (and none too observant, a form of self-preservation) I was aware that my father wanted to sleep his life away. It was a like blackout, a coma. He said he never dreamed.

My mother agreed it was the only thing to do. "He certainly behaves better when the boys are with him." She called my father He; something to be appeased. She knew she would have to go back sometime. But to her it was like a sentence of exile; her face darkened every time I mentioned it. She had left off coming to visit me.

One afternoon, as I returned to my room after a meeting, I found the door closed. This was highly irregular; inmates were never permitted to shut their doors. A nurse came tiptoeing up to me in the hall, her finger to her lips and pulling a long face:

"Shh!" she warned. "Your mother is resting."

"What is it? What's the matter? What happened?"

"It's all right. She's feeling better now."

I pushed the door open and peeped cautiously round into the room. It was dim, the curtains drawn. My impressively handsome mother, with her tan cheeks and beautiful white hair, was sitting up in my bed—a pillow behind her back, her knees under the covers, a magazine open on her lap. Her blouse was unbuttoned, revealing a vast expanse of black satin and boning, and she was licking her forefinger as she turned the smooth pages.

Her hair was swept upward, like a crown, a white tiara.

At the sight of me, her face crumpled and assumed a look of dark distress (as if I'd mentioned Florida). "The nurses have been so sweet to me. They gave me aspirin, brought me tea...." She held the empty cup aloft in the crook of her finger.

"How come you're reading in the dark?" I said.

"I wasn't reading." She lay back, putting out two paws and pulling the blanket up to her chin; the magazine slid to the floor.

I was fit to be tied. I couldn't get aspirin—it was not on my chart. Under no circumstances could I shut my door. And as for the nurses fetching and carrying, bringing tea, whispering and bobbing their heads and going on tiptoe—that was really the limit. Unheard of. Nurses were not very indulgent on W-3. How did she do it?

At the same time I was worried about my mother. She was convinced that she suffered from a heart condition, she "could go at any time." Tests found nothing. This convinced her all the more; her life was in jeopardy. She would show them all up at the autopsy.

I knew she had a doctor's appointment this very day at two o'clock. She pulled back her sleeve to look at her watch. It was two o'clock now.

"It looks like you should have kept your appointment," I said.

"Oh, you know they never find anything anyway."

I had guessed her secret—she is really a timid soul. Only a nature that feels itself helpless and powerless can be as persistent as she is. We exchanged our grimly humorous smiles, my mother gazing at me from the pillow with one eye open. Like a seal emerging from the salty depths, I thought, there was such a sleek, sorrowful sparkle. I think she has had a difficult life; I've done my bit.

I went and fetched her more tea and sat down beside my bed like a visitor. This was more like it; closer to the real truth of our relations. I knew that now she would go.

My window overlooked the emergency room; I listened to the panicky yelping sirens of the ambulances at night, watched the blue lights of the squad cars flashing across the ceiling. My sons were too young to be permitted on the ward, and I was not yet permitted off, so my mother planned to drive them up to the emergency room entrance, where I could get a parting glimpse of them. The station wagon drove up—two round heads bouncing in the tailgate. A light bowl and a dark bowl. My mother had given the boys haircuts of course; that was the first thing she did whenever she got her hands on them. The two heads emerged timidly, mistrustfully, looking all around, not knowing what was expected of them. They looked in general neater and cleaner than I was used to seeing them; older, more serious, in their bright shirts, new jeans, deep, pale cuffs stiffly rolled up. They stood side by side, holding hands.

The boys have always been close; their father and I were divorced when they were babies, and the shunting around has made them closer, fast friends. The older boy loved his younger brother at first sight, he never seems to have felt any rivalry. I was the one who felt it. Looking at the red-faced infant in my arms, with his tottering black head and squeezing fists, I was amazed that anyone could have such audacity—to demand an equal place with his brother in my heart.

At the sound of my voice, both heads lifted at once. It was plain from the expression on their faces that they had recognized my voice but didn't know where it was coming from. I knocked on the bars to get their attention. I was very close, just above them; I could see their eyes moving in their upturned faces. But the more I knocked and called and pushed my face against the screen, the more they turned their heads and raised their eyes, wondering at the source of the voice, sweeping the tall stony face of the building. I knew it seemed all windows.

My mother stooped down, prompting them: wave at your mother. Two sleeves came up, hands paddling up and down. They got back into the car, looking around over their shoulders all the while and waving. As the car drove off, I could see the two heads together still looking out, two pairs of dark frightened eyes still searching all the windows. The hands still mechanically waving. I knew they'd never seen me. They must be wondering now if they ever would. It was a terrible thing I had done to them. And I felt like a ghost.

IV.

Of course there was Fran. It was her third time on W-3; she had her cycles. Fran ran a decorator shop in Rockford with her husband—wallpapers and draperies. She was small and lively with large, dark, exaggerated features and coarse black hair vigorously sprinkled with gray. She smelled of bright red lipstick. This was the high end of her swing.

But at the low end Fran was a sloth in a smelly woolen bathrobe. Huddled, inert; she didn't wash for weeks and her hair was witchy. When she reached this point it was time to bring her in. She sat on her bed in a state of torpor. She wouldn't take a shower, wouldn't comb her hair. Forced to attend our meetings, she would retreat to the same corner of the sofa—it was her burrow—looking out suspiciously through wild strands of hair. She was present, no doubt about that. Given a variety of tasks—our work assignments, sorting laundry, cleaning up the kitchen, straightening chairs—Fran failed to perform them. Nominated for office—we held elections perpetually—she refused to run. Duly elected (it didn't matter if the candidate begged off, pleaded, even broke down in tears; these were the ones who needed it most, it was always understood whom to vote for), Fran declined to serve. She turned her face aside and shrugged, and her chin grazed her shoulder.

After a few weeks of this sort of badgering: the nurses literally shoving her into the shower—one got right into the stall with Fran, who was huddled timidly under her plastic shower cap, to make sure she stayed put; our morning rounds centering on whether Fran had put on lipstick/removed her shower cap (once she had added this item, it couldn't be detached; she looked like an air-raid warden slouching about in her helmet and mannish bathrobe); our evening meetings devoted to discussions of how come Fran, as recording secretary-elect, was failing to take notes of the discussion, suddenly Fran would begin to perform her tasks. With much energy. Patients' meeting would come to a halt while she made everybody repeat what they had said—so she could "get it all down" with her jabbing pencil. Her notebook perched in her lap at all our meetings; it was hard to persuade her to stop interrupting and trying to take minutes. Even when she wasn't supposed to. Her black eyes darted aggressively under the shower cap; she didn't want to miss a thing.

To outward appearances anyway, there seemed to be almost no interim: the transition was abrupt, total; once it got started, Fran's progress was not to be detained.

She was elected activities director. It was her job to rouse us to our evening's recreation. At least this was how Fran interpreted it. She took it upon herself—marching up and down in the corridors after dinner in new white sneakers, her hair rolled up on curlers like spools of wire, pounding on all doors: "Are you coming or not?" she'd say.

This was a challenge. Meals and meetings required attendance, but participation in recreational activities was voluntary—inmates tended to ignore them. It was always a matter of persuasion.

But Fran demanded an answer right then and there, raising her pencil.

"Well? Yes or no? What's it gonna be?"

You had to make up your mind for her on the spot, so she could mark you down at once—with terrifying finality. Yes or no had a great power in Fran's hands, waiting with the pencil. That is, it meant, yes or no. This we were not used to; not in our own lives, immobilized by indecision; not on the ward, where equivocation was the rule.

The thing was, we hated recreational activities. They were dismal beyond belief.

A walk was scheduled for every afternoon but usually failed to materialize. There was some rule about numbers; there had to be enough patients to justify sparing the staff member who would have to go with us. But it was pretty hard to round inmates up, get them and keep them together for anything. And when we did manage to get up a quorum—then we would have to take Charlotte along. Charlotte, in her cruelly heavy wheelchair. Charlotte liked to get outdoors, too.

Charlotte had jumped out of a window the year before; she was already an inmate of W-3 at the time, the Furies were after her. Now she was wheeled down from orthopedics in the clumsy old-fashioned chair, bottles strung upside down on either side. High backed, heavy armed, wooden—it was like a coach. And in its depths a timid, tiny black woman with a small pointed face and brittle legs, lingering in her braces. Occasionally she participated in the life of the ward, taking meals at the end of the long table, handling her knife and fork with difficulty.

Once she leaned out of her coach and asked me in her small frail voice, looking all about and whispering behind her hand— if I liked to play bingo. Then I overheard her asking someone else, and then another. I couldn't figure out why she kept on asking everyone the same question, in the same stage whisper. It turned out that she had been given the task of planning our evening activity and was desperately racking her brains for some solution. But we didn't know this beforehand, and almost everyone must have given the same answer, because we didn't play bingo.

Charlotte lived for these walks. As soon as it appeared that we were actually about to go, an attendant was sent to fetch her and came rolling her out of the elevator, shoving the big chair with grim-faced effort. It was impossible to lift this chair down stairs or even to lower it over street curbs; the jolting would have snapped her like a glass snake. All we could do was march along at a snail's pace once or twice around the block, the tall hospital buildings full of windows, the busy, glittering parking lots. And even at this sedate rate of progress, the liquids were splashing and swaying in the bottles suspended over her chair. I watched their motions. Alarming! Every bump, every stone, every crack (there were so many in the grimy sidewalks) was felt, conveyed. It made me wince; it set my teeth on edge. I would murderously wish that we had been able to leave Charlotte behind this time, that we could soar far, far away from her. Why should I be trapped in her chair?

But what difference would it have made? Where could I have gone? This was the essence of all our activities. We were all dangling from the same hook.

In the evening there might be a session of role playing. A pair of graduate students in blue jeans came in to supervise such games. We were assigned the task of playing rabbits and turtles. The sorrow of such an assignment was not lost on anyone, not even the graduate students. Alternatives were just as dreary. On-ward movies, old industrial shorts out of a free catalog. Pasteurizing milk, smelting pig iron, that sort of thing. Mutinous stuff! The film kept breaking, snapping, and fluttering, and the announcer's voice would grumble and lie down with a growl.

Thursday nights there was bowling in Blackstone Hall, the women's gym on campus; Friday nights was an off-ward movie.

But very few inmates participated in these activities. Going off the ward was a special ordeal.

Flora would always consent to go; she said yes because yes was easiest. She was a yielding soul. But she was also afraid to leave the ward: "Something might happen. I might never come back."

Her room was down the hall closest to the outer door, so Flora was inevitably the last one to be called for on our way out. The last stop. That was the ritual. She was a tall, pretty, redheaded woman in her forties: sausage curls, a faded powdered face, tearstained blue eyes. Knock kneed in her pedal pushers. Thus she would appear at her door, clutching her wallet and cigarettes, sweater sleeves dangling from her shoulders. Still getting ready, still combing her hair.

But Flora had changed her mind; she wasn't going.

"I don't want to go, I don't want to go anywhere. I just want to go home. Why can't I go home?"

Go. Home. To her children. She had a soft Virginia accent and she drawled the long *o*s, dragging the comb through her hair.

Now it would be explained to her that none of the rest of us, ready to go, bundled up in our coats (or, more likely, someone else's coat, one of the nurses', another patient's, a sister's, a father's, rarely our own) and assembled en masse at her door— none of us could go if she, Flora, didn't go. Because of the rule about numbers. This was what was always said: "If you don't go, X, then Y and Z can't go either. You'll be spoiling it for them." Actually, few of us wanted to go—no one really wanted to do anything—but we had been persuaded, finally, in this way, and now it was our turn to help persuade Flora.

"Come on, Flora, you're spoiling it for everyone else."

Spoiling what? We didn't know. Persuasion, however, was the name of the game, and Flora was persuadable.

This was one of the mysteries of life on W-3; there were

some inmates who could say no, indeed say nothing at all, and they would be left alone—no one would bother them, gang up on them, try to coax them to do anything. Flora was not one of them.

"I don't want to go. I'm afraid to go. I'm afraid something will happen and then I'll never go home. Oh, why won't they let me go home."

This was panic, the same panic that governed my life like a leash. A collar that jerked round my neck. How many times had I stepped out my door, only to feel myself pulled back in that way—motionless, directionless, gazing at the door lock (which had been painted over so many times), wondering where I was going, what was about to happen to me, if I would ever return? There seemed no way of knowing. Life was hazardous, without purpose or plan. Setting foot into the long dingy hallway with the carpet runners so dirty you couldn't guess the color, I might have been taking off into the next world, hell, the past, the moon. I lived in a constant state of panic, my blood was suffused by dread, it felt like battery acid. But I did not know it was panic, I had never called it by name, had never thought of using such words in connection with myself.

"Come on, Flora, don't you want to have fun?"

A mournful proposition. But by now I was really impatient with Flora, we all were, whether we wanted to go or not. We were not weeping and whining and wiping the backs of our hands under our noses. No, that was Flora. A very simple distinction. Vital. The more she wept, the softer she became. Her powder was melting down her cheeks, her blue eyes looked dim. She was taking in these facts herself, glancing at her damaged makeup. Because even Flora knew that she would end by going. Everybody knew it.

Ooo. Ooo. Ooo.

In the meantime we stood in full view of the thick glass door and the busy corridors that opened beyond W-3. Carts clanked, elevators slid open, voices piped over the intercoms. Every other corridor of the hospital really was like a thoroughfare—as heavily trafficked as any business street. But we were not part of this urgent, bustling life; we were forcibly cut off from it by that door—which opened and shut with the trip of a rifle hammer.

This was the proposition: If I felt swayed by Flora, moved by her tears, wanted impulsively to leave her alone—then I was identifying with her helplessness, weakness, panic—I was sick. But if I went along with the group, enforcing its collective pressure, bearing down on Flora, bullying her like this—what was I? At such times it seemed to me that I was standing on the threshold of two worlds, and neither was particularly desirable. All the hours of manipulation, ambivalence, our own uncertainties and hesitations were now concentrated on Flora—the soft underbelly of the ward.

Very well. At last Flora gives way, the group prevails. She'll come along quietly, biting her lip. It looks like we're going somewhere! But if the elevator does not chance to be standing right there, open, ready to receive, another crisis will develop; someone else will decide to turn back. Imitating Flora. It's too late for that sort of thing now though, you can't get away with it anymore—it's been done already. Besides, here comes the elevator. The door is sliding open.

"You know this is really crazy," Zelma remarks in her barking voice, looking all about as we crowd to the back. The elevators are big as boxcars, have to accommodate carts and corpses. "A bunch of people going bowling, and nobody really wants to!"

Who is Zelma? That's what I always ask myself. Her eyes blaze like some cold undiscovered element. But she's right—it's crazy. Nobody really wants to go. We forgot all about that— too busy coaxing poor Flora. We're being forced, that's what it is! Packed into a boxcar like cattle! In a panic, we break for the doors. But it's too late—the doors are sliding shut. The nurses shove against us. The doors close. Down we drop.

I had perhaps special feelings about visiting my old haunts; for I had been a student on this campus myself once upon a time, and the tall pointed buildings, the grassy walks we were herded along, were only too familiar and all too alien to me. The big gloomy old carcass of Blackstone Hall—where we bowled in the basement—was almost unchanged. The same high-ceilinged Victorian interior, dark wooden staircases; window seats; frayed oriental carpets, varnished oil portraits in every nook and cranny, gilded frames and potted ferns. The tall mirrors were tarnished and full of distortions, like looking at yourself in a spoon. There was the same sound of basketballs rebounding from the smooth floorboards of the gym.

There were two alleys; it took forever. Flora had to be persuaded all over again each time her turn came. "Come on, Flora, roll the ball, don't keep spoiling it..."

I used to take fencing in one of these rooms, piled with sweaty mats; a dozen girls in shorts, in tight padded jackets that fastened at the side, snorting in our masks. I always tried to fence with the same partner, a girl who shared my sentiments: cowardice. While the air rang with the clash of foils, thudding heels, the two fakers stood and poked at each other, and you could see our faces flinching inside the wire helmets. The fencing coach passed us on condition we never show up in his class again; his mask tucked smartly against his hip, like a spare head.

Even the guard was the same; a short, mustached man, a well-known campus character in his baggy breeches, a fixture of the place. He'd been there in my time and generations before that, and he didn't look any the worse for it either. Until he smiled—then I saw how he had aged, shed most of his teeth; his grin was ferocious, decrepit, like a stuffed tiger's. It was frightening. These days his post must be mostly honorary, anyway; there was another guard sauntering about, a campus cop buckled into his holster—a radio on one hip, a gun butt projecting from the other.

It was a strange sort of homecoming. I'd gone away to college at fifteen, a prodigy of sorts—honors, scholarships handed out to me like leaflets passed out on street corners. I graduated three years later. Now a dozen more years had passed—and I was going bowling through I didn't really want to.

On movie nights it was worse. Once downstairs, we had to wait all over again, this time for a taxi. No one ever took the precaution to phone beforehand; but then no one could safely predict when we might be expected to arrive downstairs. It didn't matter anyhow; all prospect of getting to any movie on time would have vanished long since. We waited, therefore, outside the entrance of the emergency room, looking out for the lights of a taxi among the vehicles driving up one after another, like carriages to the opera.

The emergency room of the hospital was very popular on weekend nights, and even this early, the rhythm was beginning. There were ambulances, squad cars, paddy wagons. The dark hulls rose behind the headlights; the passengers made quickly for the sweeping doors.

The plate glass doors opened very rapidly, with an inward rush, to speed the progress of ambulance carts. Some of us were already familiar with these doors. I had been unconscious the first time I came through them, in my blanket. Now the rapid, propelling motion had a special significance for me. I didn't know what it was exactly. The birth canal? The portals of death? It would be nice to guess their meaning, but there wasn't much time for idle speculation. The pace seemed too quick.

It was cold; most of us were dressed too lightly. A dark

wind tossed the lights of the parking lot, made them sparkle and glitter. Gerda sat beside me, shivering on the bench. A redhead of the sandy, freckled variety, but very pale and astonishingly thin. Horrifyingly, I thought. She looked as though she should rattle. Her legs, naked as always, were white as her lips; her tiny distorted feet in ballet slippers had great projecting arches—reefs of bone.

"Aren't you too cold?" I whispered.

Gerda shrugged. Her burned arm thrust into a sleep of cotton wadding, like a muff. Everything was muffled; layers, thicknesses surrounded her. Her glance was spent. The first morning when she had turned up at rounds, noticing her look of utter defenselessness, I was prompted to lean over and touch her arm in the same way: "Are you familiar with this sort of thing?"

The heavy lids had blinked once, affirmative. In the last years Gerda had spent most of her time like this; she seemed to have made the rounds of large, bleak, purgatorial institutions.

Trudy popped up; she had decided to wander back inside. She was wearing a big orange kapok-filled jacket—like a life preserver—borrowed from an extern she had her eye on. She was always trying to get something going. (She asked the extern to go to bed with her. Why, he protested, she had the clap! It was the first thing she ever told him! Never mind, Trudy said, she was only kidding about that. Besides, he was in a hospital, what did he have to worry about? They could always give him something.) She ran around to the other set of glass doors—the ones that opened only outward—and stood behind them, knocking to get our attention. Knowing no one could reach her. The clown's face was laughing at her own prank.

Jackie, the attendant, went in after her, fists shoved into the pockets of his leather jacket. A strong black man, capable, without any fanfare. He had been at Manteno, he had coped with stranger situations.

Now Yvette took it into her head to run in too. She was a great stumbling retarded child, an albino with rubbery white skin, mongoloid eyes, kinky reddish hair, powerfully in the throes of adolescence. She loved to imitate Trudy—to outdo her, if possible. She chased off in the opposite direction. Through the various portals you could see the two girls appearing and disappearing—Trudy in her fluorescent orange jacket, Yvette thrusting her face against the glass and sticking out her tongue— while the dark burly figure of Jackie elbowed its way through one set of sweeping doors and another, trying to waylay them.

Gerda shuddered; she set her teeth on edge, her eyes rolled back; the whites slid across them like a bolt. She pitched forward into my arms. She was having an epileptic seizure.

These were some of the reasons why I—we—dreaded our recreational activities.

You had to hand it to Fran though, she was effective. She got out the vote—in her sneakers, with her rapping knuckles and snapping black eyes. All she needed was a whistle. Her voice, vibrant with authority, seemed unfamiliar at first, halloing outside my door.

I was hiding behind it, trying to make myself scarce for rabbits and turtles.

Her voice rang out confidently: "Anybody home?"

Whose voice could that be? Who was knocking so boldly? What strong, peremptory presence? A new nurse on the ward? No, it was Fran! Holding up her pencil and spiral notebook.

"D'ya mind? I haven't got all day, you know."

She was a good salesman, I'll bet, in that drapery shop; she had the knack of creating a sense of emergency, self-doubt: an opportunity once lost, to be forever regretted. And indeed, within a few days of reaching this stage, Fran would be declared ready to go—home to her grateful family. Her husband, son, daughter, and daughter's fiancé—who all piled in from Rockford once a week and sat watching TV in the lounge; shoulder to shoulder, as if they were still crowded together in the car. They all looked alike, the same large dark generous features as Fran. Even the daughter and her fiancé looked alike.

Fran's recovery wowed the other inmates who witnessed it, wowed all the doctors. (For the hospital was a teaching institution, and our doctors were new to it themselves, in training, here to observe.) A patient like this vindicated all the theories about the therapeutic effects of showers, combs, lipstick, and social activities. It was a victory for the public spirit of our "community." Fran's behavior could be accounted for by all these textbook equations—yes, yes, as the visible motions of the fixed planets could be explained by the epicycles of Ptolemy.

In due time most of us would acquire more adequate clothes; we would fatten up on the starchy hospital food, get some sleep on the carefully rationed pills, calm our anxieties or inner violence with drugs, i.e., we would "get better." And it was not that the theory contradicted the facts—it just didn't link up with them. They could have hurtled forever through outer space and never reached that point of rendezvous.

At the other end of the W-3, the dead end, the double-thick glass door was always locked. It overlooked a brief, empty corridor where a guard sat in a wire cage. This was the entrance to the narco ward, heroin addicts on methadone. So far as I know, participation in this program was voluntary; but the inmates seemed subject to all kinds of restraints and shuffled about under guard in mestizo pajamas and striped hospital robes. The dreary uniforms looked like prison garb.

Their trays came up through our kitchen, stacked on steel carts seven feet high, and once a day the remains of these meals were returned. A strange pageant: two inmates in belted robes and flapping white trousers shoving shelves of dirty dishes through the dining hall while their guard—a black with a shaved head and a ring of jailer's keys slapping against his belt—shouted at them.

"Get with it! Hup! Two, three, four! You're on! You're on!"

And they'd lean into the cart and push.

There was one fat, blowsily beautiful black woman with an easygoing nature who liked to rag this guard. She would lay her powdered cheek against the metal and bat her false eyelashes and roll her rich eyes as if his orders were giving her a thrill. She'd wriggle her great soft buttocks at him. This enraged the guard.

"Oh no you don't, my lady! Hup! Hup!"

His head seemed covered with steel shavings; you could see the bulging plates of his skull. Off they'd go—Hup! Hup!—swaying keys and flopping pajamas. My sense of smell, usually keen, was practically obliterated on W-3—too much antiseptic hospital odor—but I could feel the fumes of her Tabu stinging the back of my throat.

Maybe once a week the patients from the narco ward, eight or ten in their stripes, filed down our corridors, through our rec room, and out onto the exercise deck. They heaved weights back and forth. The autumn weather was unusually fine. To a man—black and white—with their shirts stripped off and knotted round their waists, they were of one physical type: medium height, flat hips, muscular chests, wide shoulders. It would be the build of the Deep South.

The ruddy surface was marked off for shuffleboard. Geraniums in flower boxes and a few redwood benches and tables stood about. A man stretched out on a bench and eased the weights up and down over his chest; the fat woman ran about rolling the volleyball, clowning and fluttering her loose trousers and sleeves.

Once the guard with the shaved head forgot his key to

the deck and had to go and fetch it; he left his charges waiting with his sidekick in the rec room. I had been fooling around shooting pool, occasionally sinking a shot by accident; the balls were spread out on the green baize table. The patients looked about for places to sit—the room was crowded to the rafters with all its dusty, broken-down equipment—watching me as I paced with the cue. One of the men bowed: *Do you mind?* I gave him the stick and stepped away from the table. He crouched over, gliding the cue back and forth experimentally between his fingers.

At once everybody else was up, grabbing cues, chalking up, stalking round the table in robes and pajamas. It was fire at will. The balls clicked and rolled.

The pretty, blowsy woman seized a pool cue from one of them and pranced round the table.

"I'm gonna get me one of them balls."

She leaned far over, pushed up her sleeves, twitched her backside in the wide pajamas—and flubbed the shot.

"Don't wiggle so much. You throw your arm off!"

(How we on our ward grudged one another our turns. Couldn't wait till someone missed!) She sidled round, jabbing the stick playfully at this one and that. Her bare fleshy arms were covered with small raised scars, needle tattoos. She leaned over again.

"Hey! Hey! Hey!" The sticks thumped the floor.

"Oh no you don't, my lady!"

The shaved head was at the door. The guard made for her manfully, sticking his chin out—expecting to take a poke on the end of it—grappling for her cue. She laid a finger on her dimpled chin and tripped him a curtsy. Everyone laughed; they all dropped their sticks on the table.

But the guard was not exactly satisfied. "Oh no you don't, no you don't, my lady," I heard him muttering to himself, in a sort of peevish singsong, as he stood by the door, swinging his keys and herding them through.

There was no pool table on the narco ward. No piano, Ping-Pong, lounge, TV. They held no meetings, had no passes and privileges. They were not expected, not even permitted, to wear "clothes." And yet they stuck together; they were truly a body, a group, in the sense that we on W-3 could never be. And maybe the "clothes," the "community," all the social emphasis of W-3 was really meant to prevent this from happening— precisely this; to prevent us from ganging up, closing ranks in the instinctive, elementary way: we against them.

Of course this was never totally preventable. Only on W-3 it took the form of discovery—which came for all of us sooner or later—that we were *they*.

V.

Cootie was a big young black woman with the features, the expression, of a fat baby. It was as if a flat and heavy hand had pressed down on the top of her head. She was obstinately uncommunicative. She wouldn't eat, wouldn't speak, wouldn't do anything but lay her chin to her chest and shake her head: *no*. I first saw her in action at a crowded team meeting, when Dr. Zeiss—the handsome one, the one with the large, even teeth and black Persian lamb hair—brought up her case. The rest of us sat and looked on.

"Would you like to tell us a little about yourself, Cootie?"

Eyes moved to where she sat, squeezed onto the sofa in her vivid striped duster like a coat of many colors. You could tell she was aware of this, because the dark flesh seemed to solidify, become more resistant. Looking down at her fists in her inert, ample lap.

Dr. Zeiss hesitated. She was a young housewife, he began to explain, who had suddenly become (glancing at the stubbornly lowered head), uh, withdrawn. She wouldn't cook or do anything around the house. She wouldn't even talk to her husband.

"Is that right, Cootie?"

No answer.

Dr. Zeiss's throat cartilage was sharp, protruding about his rumpled collar. "Guess that's right," he said.

Dr. Zeiss was the most ingratiating of our young doctors, with his good looks and inept, groping ways. He was always cracking his knuckles and clenching his fists. He seemed mussed, distracted, as if he belonged in a laboratory instead, fumbling with test tubes, getting chalk on his sleeves. Scribbling formulas on squeaky blackboards. Once, grinning shyly, he asked me if I had any recollection of his having visited me down in intensive care. I looked into his handsome face, puzzled, not remembering.

"I was wearing a white coat," Dr. Zeiss said encouragingly, turning out the lapels of his white coat to show me. Some clue! I had been surrounded by the proverbial white coats. But all this evidence of clumsy good intentions made me feel a squirming sort of sympathy for him.

These team meetings were very *intime*. They met behind closed doors (the pleated gray doors of the lounge could be drawn in such a way as to shut off half the room). We were crammed in, crowded together, like the checkers and Parcheesi games on the shelves; we sat on tables, floors, the windowsill. This was, evidently, a psychological space. At other times, under less intimate conditions, we discussed the general situation of our "community." *Why won't Yvette get out of bed? Should Zelma be permitted to watch her portable TV?* Here, packed in, we got more personal. Or at least it seemed we were supposed to.

Most of us had felt some reluctance, pressured, probed in this way. But no one had ever reacted like Cootie. She simply put her chins to her chest and looked at her laps. I envied such obstinate silence.

Dr. Zeiss went on. The husband was worried. Now here was a vague point. The doctor scratched his ear and cocked his head and confessed he hadn't been able to get it straight. Did they or did they not have a baby? The husband said yes, but Cootie said—?

"What did you say, Cootie? I forget."

Glancing her way out of the corner of his eye. Staff seemed to have such suspiciously short memories. Though you could believe Dr. Zeiss, he looked absentminded enough in his wrinkled lab coat.

I thought I saw Cootie bite her lip, but she did not lose ground. No, she gained it. Nothing. That's what she had said before, that's what she said now. Nothing. The dark head was lowered; all you could see were her red eyes, blinking.

By now Dr. Zeiss was speaking very rapidly against the steady advance of her silence.

Looking at Cootie, a great mass of solid flesh squeezed onto the sofa with its fists in its lap, I realized that there was also something in me that wanted not to move, not to answer, not to listen; to drown out the world with the sound of its own cries. Cootie wasn't crying—she didn't need to. But her eyes were savagely red from inner weeping.

My first time at team meeting, when Inez with the tragic Spanish face—the face of dolorous mysteries (but Inez was bawdily bowlegged, one of the comical mysteries)—when Inez pressed me to speak of my "problems," I know I felt just this way. Wanted to put my chin to my chest and nevermore say a word. Cootie was a physical, visual embodiment of that inner urge. What she was, she was—wholly. She expressed it—totally. She had stores of this unspeakable thing, rich, dark, hibernating reserves of it. All she had to do was sit there in her vivid striped robe and draw on them.

Even Dr. Zeiss recognized this; felt the force of Cootie, greater than himself, greater than the mass of bodies, faces— our enforced collectivity. Greater than all outer forces. At last he gave in and ceased to press her.

I should clarify: Even Dr. Zeiss. Even the staff. I don't mean to suggest that the staff was stupid, slow on the uptake, unfeeling. If it were only that simple. Wit has nothing to do with it—and alas, neither does sympathy. The staff came and went in the real world—the term in actual use on the ward, what every outsider brought in with him—and even on W-3 they did not leave off being in the real world, going about its business. And without this armor they could not have come among us. But we had no such armor, and for most of us our presence on the ward constituted an utter disruption with this thing called the real world. We were naked, undefended at last, to the psychic currents that circulated so freely among us.

It was easier for me to sense Cootie's power—for Jesse, turning his chair about underneath him and feeling in his shirt; for Simone, hands clasped above her head, angrily muttering her prayers—than for Dr. Zeiss. He did not share our lot. Though for sure it made him uneasy.

And now I have to say that aside from all that, as an individual matter and in his own right, Dr. Zeiss did seem to be pretty slow on the uptake.

The hospital was a teaching institution. Few days went by without some request for patients to volunteer for interviews before classes of medical students. It was always made clear that these interviews were purely voluntary, that they were of no particular benefit to us, that W-3 was simply fulfilling its quota of guinea pigs. And yet inmates were always willing to go, no one ever refused; it was the one thing about which everyone seemed docile and cooperative. It was easy to understand why someone like Trudy would jump at the chance—she was so flattered at any sign of attention. ("They wanna interview *me*? You mean I get to do all the talking?") Or Iris, willing to tell her story at the drop of a hat. Maybe it was seen as a diversion, a chance to get off the ward, to break the monotony of what was called life. Or maybe it was just that, for a change, we were bluntly told right out what we knew in our hearts all along—

that it wasn't going to do any good.

In these second-year classes, the medical students were always called "Doctor." They were so nervous about conducting these interrogations, the prospect of coming into contact with patients, that they would have bolted in panic or fainted dead away on the spot if they had not been called "Doctor." They were not real doctors, but we were real patients.

"Oh yes, we need someone to volunteer for an interview this afternoon," Dr. Zeiss announces one morning at rounds. It's always an afterthought.

Simone lifts her chin—tucked over her fingertips, praying— and looks quickly around, her lenses thick as bullets, to see if anyone else has their hand up. Up goes her hand.

Does Simone want to go?

Yes, yes, she's never been to one of these interviews before, Simone says, still waving her hand; talking very fast because the drugs slur her speech so much.

Fine, that's swell. It's settled then. It'll be Simone.

Dr. Lipman's starched white lab coat can be heard scraping his chair. "But—uh—doesn't Simone have an interview with you this afternoon?" he reminds Dr. Zeiss, stressing his words significantly.

Oh, that's nothing, Dr. Zeiss says, shrugging; he'll talk with Simone later in the day.

But—Dr. Lipman is hinting harder now, squinting into the smoke of his cigar—but doesn't Dr. Zeiss think that will be too much for Simone? Two interviews in one afternoon?

"I feel fine," Simone protests at once, sitting up anxiously, thrusting out her arm and waggling her fingers, as if competing for the doctors' attention. The long oval nails pale as the palm of her hand. "I feel just fine, Dr. Lipton," the thick, spluttering voice insists—more spluttering than ever in her excitement. Naturally. She always feels fine. Even when she gags on her medicine, spits it up, keels over off her chair and falls under the table—she still feels fine, doesn't need any help. The thin elderly black woman raising herself up indignantly. There was power and energy in the thick of her confusion; something ominous, wrathful, outraged.

"She says she feels fine!"

Dr. Zeiss relays the information with a bashful grin. He is so used to encountering resistance, deflecting endless excuses (isn't that what it's all about?), that he doesn't seem to realize what quarter that resistance is coming from. His chief.

Dr. Lipman supervised the training of the four young interns. But these distinctions in rank were not clear to most of us. Simone believed, for instance, that Henry—an extern, a junior-year medical student, slight and thin with a flattop crew cut and a necktie flung over his shoulder, twenty-three at most— that Henry was chief of psychiatry. He had told her this once in order to persuade her to swallow her medicine; it was getting so she always refused it, purely in self-defense. But where else could Simone have come up with such a notion as "chief of psychiatry"? There must have been such an inaccessible person, though we never saw him—and we had no need to invent him. There must have been a superstructure, a hierarchy, a system of power and deference; but all this was not revealed to us. It was dense and invisible.

What was not invisible, what was not lost on anyone, was the fact that Dr. Lipman did not want Simone to go to this interview, or indeed to any other interview. That one thing was clear, and by now everyone could see it. Simone sensed it quickly enough, sitting up aggressively, ready to defend herself.

But Dr. Zeiss still doesn't see it. He's not going to be outdone by his patient in degree of cooperativeness, he's even more willing than she is: "I can interview her some other time then. It's all right with me."

"Aren't you a little concerned about her speech though,

Dr. Zeiss? It seems so unclear today." (As if Simone's speech were an atmospheric condition. Sometimes it seemed that way.)

Dr. Zeiss looks up, helpful to the last, painstakingly flashing his wide thoroughbred teeth. "I can understand her all right!" (Why not? The old ploy has serviced before.)

"I can talk. Oh, I can talk, Dr. Lipton, don't you worry," Simone says, shaking her chin threateningly. Something aroused, determined in her voice. Obviously this is just what Dr. Lipman is afraid of.

It is not strictly accurate to say that these interviews were of no use to us. Because you would have to tell your story yet once more, all over again. And each retelling, each repetition, hastened the time when you would get tired of it, bored with it, done with it—let go of it, drop it forever—and could soar away and be free.

New inmates were supposedly assigned a sponsor, a sort of "big brother" or "buddy"—a senior patient who would look out for you, explain things. How do you mail a letter? Buy a pack of cigarettes? Simple matters could get complicated. When are visiting hours?—that was another thing almost everyone wanted to know at first. Though visitors played no great part in our lives.

But who knows how long that institution had been moldering in neglect? Another disabled piece of machinery. The assignment of such a sponsor was left up to the patients' council—which may or may not have been functioning, it all depended—and the matter was usually forgotten altogether. Or else it would suddenly be instigated days later—when the new inmate had already spent a few sleepless nights on his camp bed, with its flat, lumpy mattress; when he had already discovered where the towels were and found his own way to meals—when he already *knew what it was like*, and had, himself, become one of those faces that would seem so dim, so strange, so inalterable, such a permanent fixture of the place to any other new inmate arriving after him. The turnover on W-3 was rapid; a few days was all it took. And yet it always seemed as if everyone else had been there since year one.

Then Simone became Cootie's sponsor.

At first it seemed to be the nurses' idea: I overheard Inez demurely explaining it (her straight thick lashes always gave her a chaste, downcast glance).

"Take Cootie under your wing," she told Simone.

Her rooky wing. There was something rooky, crow-like, about Simone. She was a folk, a spirit figure; her long bony fingers, strong wiry hair, eyes embedded in the bottle bottoms of her lenses. That night she entered the dining hall late, walking backward with stealthy, gliding steps. Her head, draped in a white towel, was bowed over her fingertips.

"How come you're walking backward?" I asked.

That piqued her. "You seen me walking backward plenty of times," she retorted, raising her head. "How come you never asked before? It's none of your business, but I'll tell you just the same."

It was Cootie. She wouldn't come into supper; she was just sitting on her bed, not budging, not talking to anyone. This was not too hard to picture: the large dark shape in the vivid robe, the fists in its lap, the chin on its chest. But Simone meant to draw her out. She took a few lurching steps backward, showing us how. Her thin arms reached out, hauling hand over hand, as if she dragged a well rope in her squeezed black fists.

"Because the Holy Ghost is with me," she said.

Uh-huh. Well never mind, it wasn't Simone's affair. The nurses would see to Cootie. Simone should sit down and eat, her dinner was getting cold. This was always seen as the ultimate in rational persuasion: your dinner's getting cold.

"Let it then!" said Simone, snapping backward over her shoulder. "What's that got to do with the Holy Ghost and me!"

And she set her back to the two long tables and lifted her hands—the palms clapped flat together—ominously above her white turban.

But after this, three meals a day, Simone really did appear with Cootie heavily in tow, in her striped duster, the coat of many colors.

"Move over, move over, make room for Cootie and me," Simone would say, hovering over the table, the dinner tray trembling in her grasp. At times she simply bordered on senility, like poor old Jesse; the loaded dinner trays were heavy, and the knives, forks, cups, covers, rattled in her rail-thin hands.

But Simone wouldn't set the tray down on any account until two places had been cleared side by side. Meantime, Cootie was loitering behind her.

"Sit down, sit down, Cootie," she'd say, turning and facing the blank, black, densely unexpressive form. And Cootie would allow herself to be maneuvered, lowered into a chair, looking down and blinking her red eyes.

"You just wait there now, Cootie—hear?"

It was pretty plain that Cootie wasn't meaning to go anywhere—spreading her knees wide and doubling her fists on her thighs. But Simone would hurry off anxiously to fetch the second tray. She fetched and carried for Cootie; she fretted over her; and as soon as she sat herself down she'd turn to her right away and start coaxing again. "Eat, eat, Cootie," she'd say.

That was one thing she could not make Cootie do, however. Cootie refused to look at her food. She became more set, stubborn, putting her chin to her chest. All you could see were her red eyes blinking.

I had to sympathize with Cootie's reaction, the way she was savagely avoiding any confrontation with the food. You got used to it; but at first it was repulsive. It tended to be starchy, gluey, wobbly, and whitish. You weren't hungry anyhow. Then you looked—just as tentatively—at the faces around you. The same surfaces, livid textures. Later on you began to take notice of the food; you noticed, for instance, that mistakes were made. You didn't get the things you had checked off on the menu. These marked menus were returned with the trays—otherwise who would remember from one day to the next?—as if to bring the matter to your attention. "Hey! I didn't get my salad!" "They gave me coffee and I ordered tea!" Or they ran out of the main dish and gave you something worse. "What do you call this?" You began to complain; the kitchen was inattentive. It almost seemed they *wanted* to confuse you, they were doing it on purpose; they were trying to make life hard for you. Nothing was an accident. At this shrewd stage (I was not spared these psychotic episodes), you took an extraordinary, surpassing interest in the food; it became a personal preoccupation. This stage seldom lasted long, and finally you just ate—everything, without looking, without complaining, without asking questions. In fact, the whole matter of food worried me in an entirely different way later on—when I knew that it was just as bad as it had been before, only now I was no longer particular about it and didn't seem to care.

Cootie's response summed it up.

"Cootie, why don't you eat?" Simone kept after her in a disappointed voice. Her long thin hands fluttered over Cootie's tray, lifting the warming covers off their plates, displaying—enticingly—the contents.

"Soup, here's soup for you. And tea. A nice cup of tea, Cootie. How about that? And here—what's this?"

Cootie wouldn't look up.

"*What's this?*" Simone repeated, suddenly angry, the way she got when things confused her. They were always trying to confuse her. And sometimes it really was difficult to determine what was on our plates.

"What were we talking about?" Simone demanded, vexed, peering through her thick spectacles at the obstinately earthbound Cootie in her many-colored robe.

But Cootie made no reply; just kept looking down and blinking her bloodshot visceral eyes.

"So you won't talk, huh?" Simone said, as if she had noticed this phenomenon for the very first time. And she gave up and turned to her own tray, briskly poking her knife and fork.

"All right for you, Cootie, that's good food."

At once Cootie lifted her head. She wouldn't eat, but she watched Simone, every movement, with her savage red eyes.

This made Simone nervous. "What you want to watch me for, Cootie? How come you don't eat yourself?" she complained, bending over her tray. Her glasses seemed about to plunge into her plate. Meantime the heavy, motionless, dark baby face blinked steadily beside her.

Simone sighed and shook her head.

"Cootie, Cootie. You just going to waste away."

Things used to be more organized. At one time the average stay on W-3 had been a matter of months; offices were held for four-week intervals in patients' council; inmates organized activities, made all the rules, even held trials for infractions. (Halcyon days. Maybe they all got some sleep? The first rule I'd make.) To hear Maurice telling of this—he'd been here periodically in the past—or Lil, the fat double-chinned majordomo of occupational therapy, you would have thought it had been some sort of health club. (And that must have been when all the expensive, broken-down equipment in the rec room was purchased.) The good old days; the golden age. I began to wonder if every "community" had such history; if they all evolved backward, into chaos. For that certainly seemed to have happened on W-3.

Now the average stay was reckoned in weeks; offices in patients' council constantly changed hands; we were ever in the midst of our weird election campaigns, half the candidates begging for defeat, weeping and imploring everyone else not to vote for them. Admissions were abrupt—emergency cases entered through the sweeping glass doors, welfare patients from the tinder-dry ghettos surrounding the hospital, their problems immediate and explosive. And the state paid for a stay of twelve days. During that time, lives had to be reconstructed.

Even the situation of the staff was temporary; they were all in varying stages of apprenticeship. Psychiatrists, psychologists, chaplains, social workers—all down here on a visit, gazing upon us as from an operating theater. Until finally you got down to the externs, junior-year medical students; teams of four or five, a flurry of white coats, assigned for a month at a time to W-3. Then they moved on to the next service: pediatrics, obstetrics, osteopathy. It was all part of their tour of duty.

Only the nurses and aides, outstaying all the rest, provided some sense of continuity, the same faces day to day. It was no wonder that the emphasis of W-3 was all on appearances—the outer world, the macroscale, the pressures of society. The ward was like a way station, an infirmary, a camp hospital: patients had to be patched up as quickly as possible and returned to the front.

In twelve days Cootie would be out.

Evidently Simone had not understood the extent of her responsibilities as "sponsor," but that lapsed institution had never been such a success! Everywhere the two friends appeared together, walking their invisible obstacle course: Simone stumbling before, leading the way, Cootie rolling after like a cannonball.

Simone tried to keep Cootie entertained. If we were idling about on the redwood benches of the exercise deck, stretching our legs in the sun, Simone, spying the long-necked sprinkling can, would spring up and clap her hands. "Let's water the geraniums, Cootie!"

It was a long golden autumn; the weather was faultless; there was an earthy smell from the window boxes. Our nurse looked up from her rug. That was an idea! Maybe we all wanted to water the geraniums? We were always lacking for something to do.

So we all picked ourselves up and waited in a queue and the can was passed from hand to hand. Cootie's head watching omnisciently over Simone's shoulder. The water dripped and sparkled from the nozzle, the bright drops fell on the thick red blots of geranium blooms. We had to be careful, conserving, so everyone could get their turn. There was plenty of water, but only three geraniums.

Simone's mothering of the younger woman appeared to be contagious. Even the nurses adopted a watchful, protective attitude toward Cootie.

"Move the table, move the table," Blanche cried, opening her mouth tarnished with braces. Cootie—incommunicado in her striped duster—had made as if to rise.

"Move the table so Cootie can get out!"

Cootie was always getting stuck behind the table.

Maurice, in his wrinkled pajamas and loose-backed slippers, got up and began tugging and lugging at the corner of the table, his yellow wattles trembling. Meanwhile, Cootie, who was built like the Minotaur, could have delivered such a message with those haunches—the merest afterthought of hip or thigh—as to knock the table skidding down the corridors. She stood, head lowered in brutish silence.

Staff seemed so encouraged by the interest Simone was taking in her charge that they moved Cootie to a room directly across the hall from her, which happened to be the one next door to mine. Why not the same room? Well, Simone had certain difficulties at night, like Jesse with his bubbling oxygen machine. Sometimes you heard feet rapping the floor; this was her way of getting stern with the devil. She would sit up primly on the edge of her bed, her hands folded in her lap, toes tapping away. She was letting him cool his heels; wouldn't give him the time of day.

Henry, the extern, had arranged a meeting for the very same night. "Got something hot on!" I overheard him telling one of the others. "A bull session with Cootie, Frankie, and Simone!" Henry was the one who had told Simone he was "chief of psychiatry."

These externs were the bane of our existence. W-3 was a soft touch, and most of them were content at least to ignore us, to come around for the free food, or to rack up a few games at the pool table; but every once in a while you got one like Henry, who wanted to do us some good. And these without fail were the worst.

I was sipping a cup of coffee and minding my own business when Henry came springing up like a grasshopper, quick strides, flattop crew cut, necktie flying impatiently over his shoulder. He sat himself down right next to me and clapped a hand on my knee. "How'd ya like to go to a movie tonight?" Sticking his chin over my shoulder to see what I was reading. It was a newspaper, a local tabloid I had swiped from the nurses' station. The black headlines attracted me. Any news was a rarity on W-3; there was an election campaign going on, but you wouldn't have known it. I wasn't really reading, to be sure, but I didn't know that either. I had picked up the paper out of habit, the way a smoker reaches for a cigarette, sticks it between his lips. I was just turning the pages.

"I can't go if you don't go," Henry went on, still snooping over my shoulder. "If you say no you're spoiling it for me…"

It was as if there were some unwritten law! No Do Not Disturb signs on W-3. As a matter of fact, there was such a law. How could we be left to ourselves—our own worst enemies?

Henry entered into the spirit of things. I wondered if he thought he was on commission—or some sort of bounty hunter—turning us in at so much a head.

The bull session took place in Cootie's room, next to mine; I saw them as I passed. All three women were sitting on Cootie's bed. Frankie was leaning her head against the wall—propping it up, as if for support; it seemed heavy, immobile, under its crooked lid. Her arms, bare to the shoulders in her sleeveless summer blouse, hung limp at her sides. Next to her was Simone, her head draped in a white towel; and on the end, perched heavily at the edge of the blue cotton bedspread, sat Cootie in her familiar striped robe.

Henry sat cross-legged on the floor. The room was dimly lit by the orange-shaded desk lamp; in the farther bed you could see the indentation of a head on a pillow, a back under a blanket turned away from the door.

I got into bed, but I could still hear them talking. There seemed to be no reason why they should ever stop. The conversation was going round and round in circles, repeating itself, stuck, caught in some groove. I could hear Simone's thick, spluttering voice; then Henry, sharp, trying to interrupt; then Frankie, protesting. She struggled to lift her head and open her mouth. Then she'd give it all up, subside, and her shoulders would sag against the wall.

They were trying to arrange for Frankie's admission to a halfway house. This term was like the drugs, it struck terror in me—I didn't want to go halfway. To be stranded forever in this condition—the eyes, the lip, the cocked wig; the face struck out like a canceled stamp. Later on I saw a photograph of myself taken during this period of my life, seated—of all places—at a nightclub table. It was only from the back. There were the grins, the flashing ice cubes in glasses, the waiter's bright cuffs; someone's thumb snapping a cigarette lighter; and planted in their jolly midst was this stranger's back, hunched shoulders—a heavy hump. I looked like a tombstone. I was struck with my resemblance to Frankie, her way of sinking her head over the phonograph.

As I lay on my back, eyes open in the dark, the whole scene in the next room was vividly before me; Frankie's face was hanging over me, listening. The open lips; the tongue loosened, disconnected, off the hook. The whites of her eyes were thick as yolks; they shone in the dark. Her face seemed swollen, it was blowing up like a balloon. All around her swarmed other faces, with a dark resemblance. They seemed to be lit from beneath, as if by firelight, and I could see their shadows stirring all over the walls—lit by the same dull orange glow. I was having some gorgeous hallucinations, listening to those voices.

They went on and on, wretchedly, peculiarly oppressive; it was like being in a fever; lit deliriums. It seemed to last for a very long time. That impression at least was accurate; Henry mentioned the next day at rounds that it had gone on past three.

The next morning Simone did not come in to breakfast. She had been busy from an early hour packing her things; she had decided to leave us. Her suitcase was ready, strapped and buckled on her bed, and Simone herself was sitting on top of it, guarding it, her raincoat across her lap. She wore a white straw hat, a little pillbox with a stiff veil; this was the hat she wore to church on Sundays, and slung over her elbow was the white patent purse she liked to carry. Staff kept going in and out of her room.

"Come on and eat, Simone, your breakfast's getting cold."

She paid them no attention. Nothing doing. She sat straight and prim as a furled umbrella, and on and off there came— we heard it all through breakfast—the familiar drill: the sharp erratic tapping of her toes.

At rounds (for life went on as usual, life always went on on W-3—that was its sharpest, bitterest, most bracing medicine), it appeared that Frankie too was in some special state. She had a dulled, preoccupied expression, holding her face in her hands. Her jaw was slack, her cheeks looked jowly; she kept poking around the back of them as if she thought she had the mumps.

It was a headache, Frankie said, stammering and interrupting herself. She had an awful headache. It had all started the night before in Cootie's room because everyone was talking so much, too much, all at once and they wouldn't let her in. Every time she opened her mouth, the words flew away. Like now. *What was it? Where was she?* Oh yes, the headache—it was because of the faces. *What faces?* That's what she would like to know; there were strange dark faces all over the room. She saw their shadows on the ceiling. She was frightened, her head was pounding; all she wanted to do was ask what they were doing there, but no one would let her. Her head felt swollen, she couldn't lift it. That's how it still felt, she said, letting her mouth hang open between her hands, feeling around her jaw.

I could sympathize. Frankie didn't seem so confused to me; I could see the gleam of coherence, like the whites of her eyes. I was a witness. I had been powerfully troubled myself, and I was only in the next room! It's odd that the one thing that never occurred to me at the time, the simplest explanation, was that I really had been seeing the same things Frankie saw. Whatever that was—some third thing, some objective fact. I'm pretty sure it had something to do with Simone. Maybe those were her spirits? Maybe they were the voices she heard buzzing in her head? This might be Simone's workaday world. And I was getting it all secondhand, through Frankie.

Whatever. In the meantime Simone sat on her suitcase, her hands folded atop her raincoat, tapping her toes. The drill was irregular but persistent, like the noises of a woodpecker, and it carried effortlessly all through the ward.

Cootie was the only one who seemed unaffected by what had gone on the night before. She sat on her bed in her striped duster, her face turned bleakly toward the hall, apparently watching the comings and goings in Simone's room. Silent, unbudgeable, unreachable as usual.

But sometime during the day—I don't know how it happened, it was as if she had been hoisted by a crane, the impression of her own immobility was so powerfully intact—there was Cootie in Simone's room, sitting on Simone's bed. The same dark expressionless outline, occupying the same corner, the head turned in the same direction. The red eyes were blinking in her large black face.

Simone seemed to have taken a vow of silence. All her possessions were assembled. It looked like she was ready to leave. But leave for what? Where? Who was coming for her? She had no home, no place to go to. They were trying to get her declared a ward of the state. At meals, as soon as she had put down her tray, she'd take her change purse out of her pocket—it was flat, depleted, utterly empty—and set it on top of her water glass. She got incensed if you asked, but that was all she was waiting for: it was a hex, she'd say; it meant that the hospital was going to go broke, end up on charity like she was. And from time to time, coming to herself, recollecting her situation, she would seize the little clasp purse in tightened knuckles and shake it wrathfully over her head.

The more staff tried to dissuade her, reason with her, the more Simone clicked her feet and pressed her lips together under her short white veil.

Cootie's face turned toward her steadily, inert and blinking. This was the way she always watched Simone at meals—very disconcerting, like a cow switching flies.

At last Simone threw back her veil and turned her face

sharply toward her friend: "What—what—what you want to keep looking at me for, Cootie?"

That night lying in bed I heard an unfamiliar voice—uncommonly sweet and clear as a bell: "Simone, honey, come on in here."

That still, small voice belonged to Cootie.

Now Cootie began to eat; she sat on her bed stitching an apron she was making for occupational therapy, humming to herself with a small complacent smile. She thumped the blue bedspread—Simone must come and sit beside her. Cootie was not content without Simone. Nightly from my bed I could hear the two women chattering back and forth across the hall like schoolgirls in a dormitory, Cootie calling out gaily in her light pure voice:

"Simone. Come say good night to me."

"Simone. Don't forget to leave your light on, honey."

"Simone. You come give me a kiss good night, Simone."

Her lovely voice had a ringing quality that carried. Regrettably you heard it only eavesdropping; Cootie spoke to no one except her friend. And at that, it seemed, only to summon her.

"Okay, okay, I'm coming," Simone would mutter indistinctly as her footsteps scurried across the hall. But sometimes they weren't quick enough.

"Simone! You get yourself right in here you, Simone."

Simone's absence was unbearable, not to be tolerated for a minute. Cootie sat up and thumped the bed.

"What you want to make me keep coming to you for, Cootie?" Simone asked, stumbling and shaking her outthrust head.

Cootie was assigned a work task—straightening the lounge. First thing in the morning, as soon as they got up, still in their bathrobes, Cootie and Simone would turn out with rags and brooms and start setting the place to rights. Early rising was the rarity on W-3; even the lights weren't up yet in the gloomy corridors. Cootie's long nightgown dragged and trailed; her head was bound in a white towel like Simone's, and she crooned to herself as she went about her task, her lips pressed in a small complacent smile. They righted the chairs, shuffled and rearranged all the piles of magazines, emptied the ashtrays always overflowing, thrust their dustcloths and brooms; and the lounge really did look less dingy when the two of them got through with it.

That white turban was especially becoming to Cootie, made her look matronly—big as she was—solid, formidable. I began to see her in a new light: a large striped hausfrau, bossy and efficient.

It got so Cootie and Simone couldn't wait until next morning; they got busy at night. As soon as we were finished with our bedtime snacks, while the straggling lines were forming outside the nurses' station, they would reappear in nightgowns and robes, their heads turning restlessly in their white turbans. And they would begin to move through the lounge in their familiar tandem formation—dusting, sweeping, dumping ashtrays. No one paid them much attention. Other inmates would be sitting around staring at the TV screen, waiting for the sleeping pills to take effect. It didn't seem to make much difference whether the set was on or off.

I don't think anyone actually watched TV. But it was there; it droned, it flickered, it made a certain bid for your attention. It was also habit—instinct, practically; phototropic. The plants turned their faces in that direction. I know for myself that it was too troublesome to watch it; there was no continuity, one image jerked noisily after another. This must have been a reflection of my own mental condition. It seemed too bizarre.

Davy Jones liked to position his chair directly in front of

the television set, about five feet away, not so much looking at it as confronting it, his arms folded across his chest. His legs outstretched—bare, hairy in his short white judo robe, thick and red like the rest of him. He wore matching terry scuffs and there were matching flecks of lather in his ears. The robe and scuffs were obviously a "get-well" gift, practically still wrapped in cellophane, like everything else he wore. His mother and sister were forever lugging armloads of plastic bags from the cleaners.

Cootie and Simone bustled back and forth. Simone was sweeping under Davy's chair, clasping a broom like a pitchfork. Cootie, crooning industriously, was leaning over, tilting her dustrag at the TV set; the prow of her hips in vivid stripes hid the screen.

Simone asked Davy to pick his feet up. He dug in his heels and stuck out his lip and stared across his folded arms. All of a sudden he changed his mind. He doubled up his legs and shot them straight out in front of him.

Cootie's head raised up in its white turban; she looked around reproachfully, blinking.

"What—what—" Simone began to splutter indignantly. "What you want to go and kick Cootie for?"

"I didn't kick anyone," Davy mumbled at once with a cunning smile, his chin on his chest. "I just picked my feet up the way you asked me to."

Simone's speech was incoherent by now, a calamity. Most inmates just gave into the drugs, there was no contest; with Simone, you felt the struggle. Her voices confused her, the drugs thickened her tongue: these were the powers she was contending with when she talked so fast.

Cootie looked on with her small, complacent smile—the way she always regarded Simone now, never took her eyes off her, even when Simone slipped off her chair and fell under the table.

At last she summoned her peremptorily.

"Simone! Hey you, Simone!"

Her voice was shocking—scathing—like ground glass in sugar.

I was shooting pool in the rec room when Simone entered in her raincoat and small white hat and veil, the white purse dangling from her elbow. As usual she seemed to be sweeping an unsteady path for Cootie, who did not fail to follow—her head rising over Simone's shoulder. Her eyes were clear and bright in her dark face; she wore crimson lipstick, a navy dress with a corseted bosom, and a handkerchief was tucked up her matronly sleeve.

It was Sunday, they had just come from church.

"Can we play too?" Simone asked, putting her purse down and springing to the table. "Come on, Cootie, let's learn to play."

Cootie sternly lowered her head. She turned around, flicked her handkerchief over the piano stool and sat down, crossing her arms.

Simone picked up a cue and poked it around a few times, leaning close over the table in her summery white veil. "How do you hold this thing now?" she wanted to know, crouching and sliding the stick between her fingers.

Cootie jealously looked on.

"You aim at that white one," I told Simone.

"The white one? Oh, where?"

The balls lay tightly clustered; Simone crouched and shut one eye and brought the stick down like a pump handle. It scarped the cloth, bounced off the cue ball, which socked into two other balls and nudged them into the pocket.

"Look at that, Cootie! Just look what I did!" Simone jumped up and down, clapping her hands.

"You get another turn now," I told her.

"Another turn! Oh, this is fun! Come on, Cootie, what's the matter with you? This game is easy! Why are you always such a stick-in-the-mud?"

Cootie adjusted her forearms across her bosom, shoving the wadded handkerchief up her sleeve.

Again Simone danced around the table, making a big circle with her long fingers. Again she shoved the stick, caused a general commotion; the balls collided; two more rolled away and sank into the corner pockets.

It took me about an hour to sink four balls.

"Oh well, Simone, it looks like you get to go again," I felt obliged to say.

"Again! Oh Lord! Oh no! You hear that, Cootie? Oh, this is too much!" She clasped her hands and plunged them to her breast. "Oh come on, Cootie. Think how pleased your husband will be when you tell him you learned to shoot pool in the hospital!"

Cootie's lips compressed in her small, complacent smile. Was it the least bit lenient?

"I'm just wondering"—Simone suddenly set the cue down on the table—"I'm just wondering if it ain't right to shoot pool on Sunday."

"Not right! Why? What's the matter?" I glanced at Cootie. There was a gleam in her eye; she gave a silent heave of laughter.

"The Lord might not like it. It's his day."

Now it was my turn to start coaxing and urging Simone to play. Not that I really wanted her to—not after she'd sunk all the balls—but coaxing, countering resistance, no matter what, was so much the way of life on the ward that everyone got into the habit; even the inmates picked it up and used it on one another. It was very persistent. Simone herself was a good example of this—although in her loyal, hovering attentions to Cootie (that constant chanting of her name!) there was something genuine and solicitous that had not come through imitation.

"Oh come on, Simone, there's no harm in it," I said, leaning my hip against the green table and chalking my cue. Actually, I didn't know but what she was right, our souls were all in peril. In fact, I was pretty sure of it.

"It's all right."

"No no. Something telling me it ain't." Simone shut her eyes fast and clapped her hands above her head. She paced this way up and down in her raincoat, moving her lips. She seemed unmindful of Cootie's presence. "Oh I was a sinner," she muttered. "I smoked. I dranked." Her eyeballs bulged like muscles under her thick lenses.

Her head bowed over her fingertips, her eyes still shut, she wandered fretfully out of the room.

Cootie was deserted. Simone had never left her flat before. She rose at once, reaching for Simone's purse—Simone had forgotten that too—and slid it over her arm. With a small smile, her arms crossed grimly upon her broad chest, she pursued—silently, relentlessly, like the dark side of the moon.

The impression was unmistakable. Cootie was a keeper.

"Pray for me, what's-your-name," I heard Simone mumbling to herself as I lay in bed. That startled me. Was *what's-your-name* one of her designations for the deity? I knew she was on pretty close terms...

"Pray for me, what's-your-name, pray for me."

Her thick, slurred voice was halfway between weariness and rage.

"What's your name!" she demanded with sudden, angry energy. "What's your name! What's your name!"

I realized that she was in the next room talking to Cootie.

On the twelfth day Cootie departed. Homebound. Bearing herself proudly in her navy dress, smelling of bright lipstick, waving her handkerchief. She seemed actually radiant. It often happened that the ones who entered in the greatest extremity would be the ones to leave first, sound and smiling. Sailing off into the sunset. While others—less demonstrative, seemingly less despairing—lingered on. This strange fact must have had something to do with the welfare statistics, those unseen bureaucratic forces. But there were other forces, far more powerful. The moon phased, the tides swooned, the fish danced—and the seeing eye signaled, the swift glass doors of the emergency room burst open, swept us in. No one knew what this was all about. Mysteriously, relentlessly, no matter what the doctors did or failed to do—these forces went on working, doing things their own way.

A few days after, Simone's own transfer came through. She was permanently committed to Idlewild, the state institution—the monolith.

VI.

Nights were the primitive hours on W-3. After eleven o'clock there was a skeleton staff, an attendant and two uniformed night nurses. One of them, Hazel, was a beautiful black woman, well over six feet, with agate eyes and golden teeth: our watchman. Every half hour a powerful flashlight swung through the corridors, entered the rooms, shone over bedclothes, faces. A strange thing: you don't see the light of course, it blinds you; you don't see anything. A moment later you translate this angry sensation: Oh. Light. Night after night I let my eyes shine back at the flashlights: *I'm not sleeping*.

I didn't sleep, and I was greatly preoccupied with the subject of sleep. But I was not alone, it was no private matter; most inmates did not sleep. It was part of our condition; sleeplessness was endemic to W-3. I began to understand this when I saw the straggling queues lined up outside the brightly lit glass of the nurses' station—inmates in robes and slippers awaiting the nightly dole of sleeping pills. The pills had to be washed down then and there—the nurses watched you swallow—to prevent fantasies of stockpiling.

I didn't take any pills. I was afraid to. I had swallowed an entire bottleful. They were transparent red capsules in a brown bottle; the last one had gotten stuck in the bottom and I pried it out, wriggling my fingers inside the narrow neck. It couldn't have made any difference, but I had been determined to swallow that one too. And now it seemed that this last oily red capsule was stuck in my throat. The impression was very distinct; every time I thought of swallowing another, I could feel the single pill sticking. It couldn't be dislodged; nothing could wash it down.

But I dreaded facing the night alone, unaided. That's what it amounted to. The sirens cried and carried on, the blue lights pumped across the ceiling. And the ward crawled with noises. As soon as the lights went out, it was as if a hand had thrown a switch; some other life took over, inmates got up, went on the move. Obviously even the pills didn't work for everybody. Every morning we heard now many cc of Thorazine had been shot in Zelma's butt, and how she had failed to fall asleep. The restless noises in the dark made the rooms seem like traps, cages, behind their big locked screens. It often seemed to me that the soundest sleeper in the world, with the most blissful conscience, would have become an insomniac here, tossing and turning just like the rest of us. So what chance did we have, with our troubled souls?

There was no rule about lights out. The staff did not like to make rules, to present us with an arbitrary authority. The myth of the community was our arbitrary authority. It made desperate demands.

Davy Jones, bare legged in his short judo robe, liked to shoot pool by himself in the dark. You could hear the balls clicking and grumbling, rolling surlily round on the table. Jeffrey played his radio around the clock, tuned to hit music; he sat on his bed cross-legged, shoulders hunched, slapping his bongo drums. Trudy played solitaire at the nurses' station. You could hear her smacking the cards down on the table, carrying on one-sided conversations at the top of her voice with Hazel, a good listener. Maurice prowled the halls on shuffling feet, making the rounds from one end to the other, trying the locked doors. He'd shake the handle, pivot about, retrace his steps. His wife had died on another ward. Those dreaded footsteps in old man's slippers dragged the corridors with fearful regularity—like death walking the floor, knowing the way.

As soon as one of these situations arose, it was a state of nature, barter and exchange. We must challenge one another directly; learn to deal with our hostilities, handle our aggressions, confront the anarchy in ourselves. In other words, these golden opportunities would never have arisen if Jeffrey's radio or Maurice's shuffling slippers had been keeping the doctors and nurses awake. That seemed to me the essential difference. I knew we were supposed to be a community by day, all one happy family—we had to humor the doctors; but couldn't we become a hospital by night, so the sick could get some sleep?

One night I got out of bed and followed Maurice down the corridors. His shoulders were rigid in his wrinkled pajama shirt; he inclined slightly backward with alcoholic dignity. He stopped at the door, tried the latch, gave it a shake—and shoved off, spinning about with a sort of flutter kick, retracing his steps. His movements seemed precisely timed; he swung his arms from side to side, wrists forward, paddling, scraping his feet. I touched his shoulder. His head gave a shake; his cheek turned, his eyes moved over my face. I looked into exhausted, wrinkled, unlit depths and saw that he was sleepwalking. So much for private enterprise. Our bargaining powers were limited indeed.

One morning at rounds, Dr. Lipman called for the sleep chart. A document was produced, a graph marked off at half-hour intervals, with checks and dashes indicating who had been asleep or awake all through the night. The existence of this document amazed me. So that's what those flashlights meant, in our faces! After this, when the lights shined I shut my eyes and pretended to be asleep. And this of course was what everyone did, sooner or later; something you learned to do. You stole a moment of privacy.

"Maybe I am crazy," Jeffrey said one morning—in his bathrobe, the soles of his big bare feet (for which he apologized) sticking forward and his black hair hanging in his eyes. "Maybe I am crazy. That's what I thought last night. I was lying in bed, listening to all those noises, and just looking at the screen—the big locked screen. And I thought, Maybe that's what I'm doing here! Maybe this is the thing that people call *crazy*, maybe this is what it means. Lying in that room in the dark, listening to the noise in all those other rooms. And here I am locked up with the rest. So maybe I really do belong here. Maybe this is what it's like, to be crazy."

I was beginning to think so too.

Day after day it continued. Morning: community rounds. Noon: team meeting. Night: patients' council.

Trudy comes stalking in with rugged steps, her housecoat whipping about her bare legs. She plops herself down, crosses her legs like a yogi on the cushions—exposing what is euphemistically referred to as "everything" but is, believe me, not so very much: a snub, smooth crotch in cotton underpants, elastic-banded thighs.

This upsets Zelma however.

"Trudy! Sit right! Cover yourself!" She squawks and flaps and screeches like a parrot perched in the corner. "It's not ladylike. It's not"—coming up with the pious formula so familiar on the ward—"it's not appropriate."

"Oh kiss my ass, Lady Godiva. Look who's talking. What do you know about appropriate. You wear your skirts up to your split."

True, unfortunately; the ropes of chains and beads round

Zelma's neck dangle past the hem of her embroidered caftan. Her cheeks are long, battered, rouged, and she's wearing a band of feathers around her head. Her eyes blaze with triumph; she loves to provoke a personal attack. "You hear that? Is that any way to talk?" she asks, looking around, shaking her feathers and rattling her chains.

"I take that back," Trudy says, rocking back and forth from one buttock to the other and flipping the edges of her skirts over her knees. "I just didn't like the way you said it."

Now that she's settled herself down so comfortably, the inevitable. She jumps up right away.

"I need a cigarette. Someone gimme a cigarette."

Just like that. Trudy doesn't wink, doesn't whisper; doesn't go through the whole ritual of signals, self-abasing gestures— catching someone's eye, raising the fingers to the lips, pretending to take a puff.... That's the way people cadge cigarettes from one another, even in a mental hospital. But not Trudy.

"I wanna cigarette."

"This is a hospital," I rebuke her, rather loftily, high and mighty, tossing my head like a tethered goat. "There are other patients here besides you."

"Tough tit."

A few seconds later I hear trotting bare feet and Trudy's face stoops down to me, all concerned, tempering the wind to the shorn lamb: "I'm sorry, I take that back. It's not that I don't like you...."

Then, whirling round, her voice rising, the veins standing out in her outstretched throat: "A cigarette, a cigarette." Pacing up and down and howling like a muezzin.

The cigarettes, of course, which burned tiny black holes on all our clothes.

For some reason Trudy liked to direct remarks and reminiscences about her sex life at Blanche—the oldest, the plainest, the most obvious virgin spinster among the nurses. She was always chumming up to Blanche, setting her tray down next to Blanche's at the table; her blond hair dipping deferentially, carrying on what she took to be civil conversation.

For example: "It's not true that Greek men take you from behind," Trudy informed Blanche earnestly, gulping down a mouthful and raising her painted eyebrows. Trudy hated slander. "I had a Greek boyfriend once and he did it the same as everyone else. You know—the man puts his mmm-nnn in the girl's unh-unh—"

Blanche winced. A registered nurse, familiar of the human body, her nameplate pinned to her breast, she was supposed to be unflappable. But her pinched face went pale; her mouth full of rubber bands and braces formed: *My word!* This was what made Trudy seek her out, light on her lackluster brow like a homing pigeon; she knew she could always get a rise—or at least a twitch—out of Blanche.

"You shouldn't talk with your mouth full, anyway. Try to chew with your mouth closed." Blanche closed her mouth and silently moved her thin lips.

Trudy picked up her fork and imitated Blanche, munching sincerely. The hospital food was intentionally starchy; Trudy was putting on a lot of weight. Her figure was getting thicker, straighter, chunky, more childish. She had no waist anymore and her arms, even her elbows, were round and chubby. This made her look all the more determined as she prowled the ward on pounding bare feet—looking for some pretext, some outlet for her soul.

Officially Trudy was still in isolation, but she seemed to have the run of the place, to come and go at will, on impulse. Maybe it was osmosis. The nurses were supposed to lock her up at night, but you'd find her in your bed instead, hiding from them, ducking her head under the covers. She helped herself to Jeffrey's bed and rolled over right on top of him. Jeffrey complained: "I'm a growing boy, you know."

She dropped onto all fours to take a peek under the nurses' skirts. She walked right in and used the toilet, squatting down without shutting the door. Another habit that upset Zelma: Trudy said she didn't like to be left out of the conversation. She didn't like to be left out of anything. She had followed Yvette into the shower stall.

Funny Yvette, with her pointed teeth and raveled red hair, folded her arms across her chest and barred the way with dignity: "I like to take my shower alone."

"I've had intercourse with forty-three men," Trudy continued, turning toward Blanche in her confiding way, but raising her voice very distinctly above the noise of scraping and banging trays. "With forty-three men. Sometimes only sucking though," she added—to be fair. Blanche's rubber bands seemed to snap.

"But I only had orgasms a few times," Trudy burst out suddenly. "Just a few times! Almost never!" And here the throat bulged, the big painted mouth crumpled bitterly; she lowered her face and hung her head. I heard her whimpering: "Never. Never."

I was stunned. This was a textbook. Can it be that she only read it somewhere? I wondered, gazing at the rows of dim faces, the scrawled sign on the wall; Trudy's shining, quivering blond head.

"You mustn't say such things, Trudy. It's not appropriate." Blanche patted her lips with her paper napkin; sympathy always made her stiffen.

It's not appropriate. The very words we heard most often— performed with reverence, a kind of obeisance, foreheads touched to the ground. And yet invariably applied, as now, with reckless inaccuracy. What Trudy had just said seemed to me all too appropriate. Like a dictionary definition, one of those thick tomes in Zelma's room; the attributes of a case history with some Latin name. It was hair raising. You mustn't say such things, Trudy, I thought, looking at her stricken, downcast face, suddenly afraid of her. No, you mustn't say such things. It can't be that your life is an open-and-shut book.

Trudy only wept for a moment though. Trudy never did anything, even weep, for more than a few minutes at a time. This was too instructive. It was obvious that Trudy was a classic case, some sort of a classic. Her self-revelations were so predictable as to leave you speechless. Trudy was not less candid with herself. But *classic* is just a nice word for *stereotype*. Could it be that the reluctance of the rest of us to express ourselves, reveal ourselves—in the same way that Trudy was everywhere and always expressing and revealing herself—was simply a fear of this? A suppression of stereotypes? If we spoke our hearts at last, would the words come out like this—like slugs of type?

A student had been admitted on the same afternoon as Guz; he had been studying too hard, was overwrought. A doctor at student health looked him over, chucked him in. Looking alarmed. At any given time there were bound to be students from the university on the ward, sallow, hairy hypes, like Ivan with his bare chest and long straggling hair and black preacher's coat; tripped out on drugs, inward, pensive, gloomier than any of us. But this one was an exception; T-shirt, gym shoes, thin dangling girlish arms, milk-white skin and freckled cheeks. His hair was ruddy, fuzzy, like a pelt. That night at patients' meeting his cheecks were blazing. He had been asked to introduce himself and everyone was looking at him.

"Peter, you want to tell us a little about yourself, Peter?"

"I don't think I belong here," he began. Glancing round at all of us, but especially, out of the corner of his eye, at Guz—sprawled in his chair, his arms propped up in bandages, his legs spread out—displaying the blood-soaked socks for all to see.

"I'm not—I mean, I'm not—"

He didn't want to say it to our faces (our strange, wan faces): that he thought we were crazy, that he could see it just looking at us—that anyone could see it. He was well brought up, for one thing, had been taught not to point and stare. And besides, it might excite us. His brown eyes were beadily on the move, patrolling, taking it all in. But at last it was simply a matter of self-defense, so he said it:

"I'm not crazy. I don't think I belong here. You people are different from me. I was just studying too hard. There's nothing wrong with me."

Basil spoke up. "You don't have to be crazy to be here," he said gently. "We all have our problems. We come here to talk about them."

Heads nodded at once. We were grateful for Basil. It was a good thing he had answered, for he was about the most presentable among us—a light-skinned Negro, well mannered, quiet, slightly effeminate, with karakul hair and a slim pencil mustache.

"Maybe. But I don't think I have *your* problems." The cornered glance swept over us again.

"Yes, sure you feel that way," Basil said. "That's what everyone feels at first."

This was true, but the boy couldn't know it. He didn't believe it. It didn't matter what "everyone" said—how could it? Everyone else was crazy.

And this too was what everyone felt, what we heard all the time. Others might be assembled for more conventional reasons—and quite evidently were, all you had to do was look around you, as this boy was doing now—but as for you, yourself, well, that was different. The reasons were special, the circumstances were mitigated. It was an individual case.

"I came here for a *rest*." That was Georgia. "*Just* a rest.

The doctors wanted to fatten me *up*." Decisively thin, dark, beautiful, hostile. She had been admitted at the same time as Jeffrey, both peculiarly beautiful young people. I thought they were brother and sister at first, even though Georgia was black. Still, the impression persisted. There was an ardent likeness; dark eyes, typical pallor, vibrant black hair. Yet each seemed solitary, and I noticed in particular that they had nothing to do with each other. They might have been on different wards, floors, poles.

Georgia was peevishly implying that because of all these other types, she was not getting much *rest*.

Then there was Pearl. When we went bowling Pearl refused to give up her turn; she'd hurl one heavy black ball after another down the alley, squatting on her haunches to look after them, see how much destruction they were doing. Punching her knees with her hard little fists. "I'm not crazy, you know. I'm just an alcoholic. An alcoholic, that's what I am. Look here—I signed myself in here." For some reason, this "I signed myself in here" was always the ultimate claim to moral distinction. And little Pearl, with her dark-muzzled face, her broad black cheeks and short thick neck, gazed round truculently at the rest of us— as though we had been rounded up with police knocks in the middle of the night.

Or: "I just needed a place to stay." That's what Zelma always insisted. "I have everything I own in the world with me—where else could I go with all that luggage?" And she really did seem to check in and out as if the hospital were her hotel.

Or there was me. Shrugging it off. "It doesn't matter, I'll be out of here by that time."

It all boiled down to the same thing: no one belonged here. It was a familiar tune, you heard it over and over; like everything else on W-3. But not everyone said it; at least not so plainly.

This was only what Basil was trying to explain in his earnest, soothing manner. His thin eyebrows working. They were as black and slim as his mustache.

Elke was nodding encouragingly; she seemed to be prompting Basil with the movement of her lips. She had a nervous habit of parroting your speech, her eyes blinking with high intensity. Elke had been admitted initially on a one-to-one: twenty-four-hour surveillance. "One-to-one" meant the ratio of inmates to keepers. I first caught sight of her peering and blinking into the brightly lit glass of the nurses' station. The corridor of the locked ward adjoined one side of the nurses' cubicle, so we would sometimes glimpse the inmates of isolation standing and watching us through that glass. Apparently our life seemed much brighter and livelier to them.

Elke, a research chemist with three small children, was irresistibly suicidal. Her hair was not so much blond as translucent, and her eyes were the same kind of light-transmitting blue. Her eyebrows were puckered and white, like something on a film negative. There was a stark, institutional look about her—the blond hair chopped off straight around her ears; hugging and chafing her elbows, her hands up her sleeves. She seemed to be wearing a sort of burlap sack. As a matter of fact, she had spent her earliest years adrift from her parents, a war orphan; and after the war, when the family was reunited and had immigrated to the States, her father, a psychiatrist, a specialist in battle psychosis, had taken a job at a grim state mental institution in upper New York. Elke had grown up on the grounds of this outpost, a fortress, its white barracks and shorn lawns visible through the spikes of the fence.

As she was meek and tractable, not one of the violent (except toward herself), Elke was permitted to take her meals out on the ward, sitting at the end of the table under the eye of her special nurse. We were all subject to constant scrutiny, but not like this—face to face. Even here she watched us as though through glass, her eyes piercing and blinking at the clatter of the trays. Her face had a frozen radiance, a space look; the cheeks burned like dry ice.

By now she had accumulated the usual grab-bag wardrobe; a pair of fringed mukluks and an ugly duster of shiny iridescent fabric shot through with metallic thread. It glittered—it fairly rattled, like sheet metal; such a din that it hurt to look at her. Were we to assume then that this getup represented the pure soul of Elke? For she was a pure soul. I had been drawn to her from the first, knew I had found a friend. Even her nervous habits seemed to spring from kindness and concern. She was anxious now for Basil to create a good impression, to say the right things, so that this boy, Peter, would calm down and be convinced. She kept nodding and blinking, knitting her brows, moving her lips. Hands reaching into the deep pocket of her duster and scratching. Her hands were covered with a scaly red rash, an allergic reaction to the chemicals she used in her lab work, and she was always hiding them and scratching on the sly.

Basil cited the irony of his own case. The rest of us believed that we didn't belong here, but he, Basil, believed that he did. Which was why he had had such a hard time convincing anyone else. He had tried to get himself admitted to the psychiatric ward on various occasions, even going so far as to take an overdose of sleeping pills and presenting himself for the services of the stomach pump. And even that didn't work. They patted him on the back and sent him home. Even the doctors didn't think he belonged here!

I have said Basil was Negro; I just can't call him black. Black he was not; but black was what he wanted to be. He wanted to rage, to revolt, he wanted that precious black right—but he didn't know how. What did you have to do to get yourself admitted to a mental ward?

Now Julius, a black man, had been dragged in struggling with three orderlies—a head taller than any of them. The head that he wanted to dash against the wall. He was thin, angular, curry colored, with cheekbones like the flat of a knife blade. They pulled him away from the walls. He clutched his head and started pulling up his hair by the handful, like tufts of grass. He could feel his brain squirming, he said; creeping toward his nose. It wanted to get out. He seized a table lamp and smashed it over his skull. No sooner did they get him locked up than we began to hear the battering in isolation, the thin partitions trembling. Julius seemed to be throttling the walls. After a while it dawned on me that he was ramming them with his head.

But this, evidently, was how! To be black, to rage, that was the only way. Only Basil did not know how to batter and rage, how to tear his scalp with his fingernails and knock his head against the wall. He had simply turned up in the emergency room, as calm as he was now (I could imagine), his thin mustache twitching, stating his own case in the same soft voice. "I'm an emergency." Basil, who was so anxious to be one of us, was the right one to talk.

And he went on talking.

We sometimes had this problem with Basil. He was so gentle, so logical and persuasive. His eyebrows so effortful, expressive. Only he didn't stop. You never knew when this was going to happen; there came a point of strangeness, a point of no return—the tongue yoked to the monotonous voice—when it dawned on you as a distinct possibility: Basil was going to talk for the rest of your life.

This point, the boy, Peter, had evidently reached; his cheeks seemed about to burst with ruddy blood, his eyes were popping. Basil was confirming his worst suspicions. This was madness! And he looked around to see if he was alone.

Elke blinked at me. We had both seen what was happening, we felt sorry for the boy. But he was here, wasn't he? That tended to contradict him. And Basil's impulse was really the impulse of the group; to engulf the newcomer, to submerge him. To make him see that he really was one of us.

This must have been why, in spite of our own boredom, the terrors of monotony (Basil could make you feel that too), no one moved to shut off the flow of speech. We all seemed to be in a trance, like Guz—gazing at his wrists.

Old Jesse swung himself up and went in search of an ashtray. I think he had been a Pullman porter; he certainly looked the stereotype: slight and frail, with his crooked back, his self-effacing stoop. But his long gnarled arms were still full of strength and he swung them with ease. At meetings Jesse was always making exchanges; suddenly his ashtray wouldn't suit him. He'd set it down, heft it, set it down again, feeling his chest for matches. Then he'd swing himself up, start his tour of the lounge, the dining room—in full view of the meeting—inspecting all the ashtrays, emptying them or not, as it pleased him. His bald black head was stuffed with cotton.

Jesse was even more particular about his chair. He arranged and rearranged it. He might put it in the center of the group, right out in the middle of the floor; he might place it on the periphery; then again, he might drag it back to the long table and decide to fetch another. Starting the whole process all over again, lugging the chairs about effortlessly under his long swinging arm, one hand groping in his shirt for matches. He never disturbed anyone; the meetings went on as usual. But Jesse might go to all this trouble, all this dragging and rearranging, only to seat himself at last with his back to the rest of us—the only satisfactory solution. That was hard to take; you couldn't help seeing it as a commentary on the proceedings. They seemed pointless enough.

God knows what Jesse made of all this—meals, meetings, faces. He saw ghosts in the dark, he had his troubles with asthma. An oxygen apparatus hung over his bed, but he couldn't be taught to use it, for he didn't trust it. Its lathered breathing gave him bad dreams.

No, Jesse was only minding his own business; and he went his own way among us, unmolested, unmolesting.

Now I watched him shuffling and shuttling the chairs at the dining table, swinging them about like baggage, looking for one that would do. At last he dragged a chair out from the table and sat down for a bit in the darkened room, grabbing a smoke. All the other chairs were lined up behind him. Fat white smoke rings came floating out, punctuated, drifting off into thin air. The tufts of cotton stuck out of his ears. His long arm moved across his chest, searching for matches. It had nothing to do with us. And Basil went on talking: it had nothing to do with him. There was no claim on Jesse's attention, no contest for his soul.

All at once Guz sat up. The movement was startling, like a lunge; he had appeared to be in a glassy slumber. And any movement Guz made was bound to startle, he was so powerful and unwieldy, an ice floe breaking up. Basil stopped talking. Everyone looked expectantly toward Guz.

More startling, Guz began to speak.

"I tried to take my life," he said, holding his taped wrists before him as if they were shackled together. "I tried to take *my life*." His big head swayed. Even the outsize hospital shirts, which swam on anybody else, were too tight for Guz; the strings bursting on his powerful neck. His throat was a spasm of muscle. And all these muscles seemed to be tightening, concentrating on one effort—speech. You could see he was not accustomed to such effort. His face was agonized; his deep voice shook. And we now discovered that Guz had a speech impediment, stuttering, tongue tied. Or else they had already doped him to the gills, shot him with an elephant gun. But it seemed he'd been listening to Basil all the while, and Basil was missing the point. So the time had come for Guz to speak.

His tongue was thick and struggling in his large honest face. I was straining with the effort of listening to him—wanting to urge him, prompt him, help him out of his difficulties. But there was no need. Speech had come over him like a witness at a séance. It was plain that Guz was telling us all about Life. And that's what I wanted to hear. The word had fresh powers for him, inconceivable. And his big body—towering, bloody, self-mutilated—seemed to have special authority on the subject. Even his mutilated speech. It was not surprising such a message should be hard to decode, that you should have to struggle to hear it. It seemed to me that we, his listeners, were the ones with the real impediments; stones in our mouths, eyes, ears.

"Sacred," Guz said. "Beautiful." "Trust." "Truth." "Communication." "Silence." Yes, but how do these words go together? Won't someone please tell me?

Apparently what had not worked for me had worked for Guz. His tongue was tied, but what had held his tongue was loosed. Wasn't that what we were all waiting for? A powerful force, a tide of emotion, strong enough to carry us forth, to set us free? His shirt was binding under the armpits, it was practically like a straitjacket; he steadied his elbows on his knees. It got worse as he went along. Guz was speaking beautiful words to us, noble, moving, uplifting ideas, but we couldn't hear them. That's all there was to it. The truth was massive and inarticulate. It was, it must remain, a personal statement. We let him talk on, just like Basil.

I couldn't help glancing over at the new boy. His face was fixed on Guz with a rapt, bright-eyed, terrified expression. The bloody black man might yet be seized by other emotions, more direct and violent. This boy was lucky, really; he was seeing madness. Something that complied with his expectations of madness. Few of us ever got to see anything like this.

Let me tell you about that thing in Julius's head.

Histories like mine, of long debilitating illness, vague recurrent symptoms, hospitalizations, were common enough on W-3; these things go together. It had been going on for a couple of years. One day, many months before, I had had a bout of something I called brain flu. All the by-now only too familiar symptoms of flu, its light-shrinking sensitivity, seemed to be concentrated in one place: my brain. I could feel it, a separate entity—an unhappy mass encased in the skull; tissue, blood, like any other organ. It felt shriveled, dehydrated. Like a caterpillar that curls when you touch it. The pain was not that great, but it was torment; you couldn't run away, there was nowhere to escape to; you couldn't go and hide from the thing squirming in your head.

It occurred to me that this might be what was meant by a breakdown.

Everyone knows what it would be like to crack up, to go crazy. A blackout, a massive power failure. The fuses will blow, the lights will blast; the cow sirens start wailing. You will stop functioning—and start screaming.

But what if it is not like that? What if the term is literal? Maybe it really is a sickness of the brain. *In the brain.* The disease attacking the actual, physical site. Maybe the mind protests its condition like any other ailing, injured part of the body: sends out the same signals, pain and retreat. I could feel it cringing, retracting, a thick gray pseudopod creeping inside my head.

I'm sure this was what Julius was experiencing when he banged his head against the wall; protesting that his brain was crawling. But I didn't recognize it then; Julius seemed too sensational for me.

I had felt like banging my head against the wall too—I remember running up and down, crying out, with my elbows covering my ears—but I called the doctor instead. It took some time to reach him; he was home sick in bed himself, poor man, down with a terrible cold. His voice was thick over the telephone. He told me right away that all I had was a cold. I insisted; I expressed my fears. That annoyed him; doctors hate it when you make your own diagnosis. And such an old-fashioned self-dramatizing diagnosis—like the heroines with brain fever in Russian novels. (I suppose that was the same thing?) He snapped out his prescription: get some Coricidin.

The strangest part of all this is that the offending term, *breakdown*, was laid to rest; it never occurred to me again, not even all the while I was on W-3.

VII.

Theoretically twice a week, less often in practice, the inmates of the psychiatric ward got to see their psychiatrists; each of us was assigned to one of the four young interns. But these interviews frequently didn't come off as scheduled; postponements were the rule, and they might be continued from one week to the next. Deronda hadn't seen her doctor in more than a month. She spent most of her time in bed, yawning and stretching in her big pink hair curlers, carrying on long and secretive conversations over the telephone. (It was a good thing she was so even tempered, phlegmatic; Yvette was her roommate. No one else could have put up with it.) She was waiting for her doctor to come back from vacation.

It didn't really matter. But we didn't know this—and there was no way of knowing it. These private conferences with our doctors seemed to be the payoff, the big bout, the main event. We believed that this business of seeing the psychiatrist was the chief business of life, its most significant feature; that we spent all the rest of our time waiting for it to happen—that this was what we were in the hospital for.

And when these appointments were canceled, we felt this all the more.

When the doctors came strolling in with their white hems

flapping and announced that they were too busy, on duty in the emergency room, had a "conflict"—there was frowning, darkening, grumbling; the prevailing mood of life on the ward. It was a setback; we had been erased. Now there was nothing to look forward to but more waiting. And we might be waiting again for nothing.

We spent all the rest of our time being a "community," talking about the "community," conceding to its claims. When would we get a chance to talk about ourselves? To be ourselves? Whoever that might be?

My doctor was Doremy, with his long legs and little soft beard on the tip of his chin, like a black cottontail. Dr. Doremy looked much younger than anyone else around, even the externs. Iris instantly sniffed this out.

"Growing a beard to make himself look older!" she declared—stroking her strong chin (so much more prominent and forceful than Dr. Doremy's). This "boy" had had the nerve to come up to her and announce that he was going to be her doctor—hers, Iris's, a woman of her rich experience, her maturity! Take her fate in his hands! Not if she had anything to say about it.

This, of course, happened right away, before Iris had more or less receded from our presence on powerful drugs; when she was still vigorously asserting her priority. And she objected to Dr. Doremy's very evident lack of it.

Iris was right, actually; it was absurd. But I liked Dr. Doremy—with his big teeth grinning through his beard, wide, irregularly spaced, like a child's second teeth. And I was glad that I had been assigned to him and not to any of the other interns. They were dullards, poor sticks; he was obviously the best of the lot. And so forth and so on. Ho hum. This was exactly what other patients felt about their doctors—from whom we expected so much. Too much.

Dr. B— was a dark and gloomy little man, Filipino, I think, with a high thickly bulging forehead and eyes that lurked in their bony sockets. He paced with his hands behind his back, shoulders heavy hunched in his long white coat. He spoke only in grunts.

"Good night!" Iris announced as Dr. B— came stalking into a meeting, his forehead jutting, the weight of the world on his shoulders. "Good night! Good night!"

Dr. B— looked up darkly. "Huh?"

"Your name in Spanish means good night!"

"Uh," said Dr. B—, glancing backward as he parted his white tails and took his seat.

That was the only time I ever overheard him actually engaged in conversation.

But the one exception was Dr. Dampier, because she was female. And pregnant—as if to grossly underscore the fact. She had passed the first trimester, the bloom was off; she had faded and thickened. A fair, heavy, dull-fleshed woman, sitting passively at our meetings, legs spread under the weight of her belly; elastic stockings. Protuberant blue eyes. This may have been the famous bovine placidity of pregnancy, but that blank creature look was familiar enough here; it seemed to have other explanations in this setting. In fact, Dr. Dampier looked just like everyone else; she was almost invariably taken for an inmate. "Is it one of *us* or one of *them*?"—that's what you couldn't help asking all the time. Our other doctors were taking no chances— they wore white coats. Inmates sometimes resented Dr. Dampier, felt demoted if they got a woman doctor.

The fact that our doctors were complete novices, trying to gain experience, was never concealed from us. But it wasn't exactly broadcast either. Iris, however, had been around mental institutions long enough to develop political instincts, and she wanted Dr. Lipman to be her psychiatrist; that was what she was angling for. He was Zelma's doctor, and he had no other patients; Zelma often said that other inmates were jealous of her because her doctor was hers exclusively—and head of the ward. She was wrong about that. For that very reason—because he had no other patients—Dr. Lipman was of no consequence to anyone else, unknown, practically anonymous. Many inmates never even caught his name, or never got it right. "Who's this Dr. Lipton?" No ears were pricked up, no eyes raised submissively at his entrances.

He was brisk enough; a compact, frontal sort of man in a starched coat, with a wide blunt forehead and shoe-polish sideburns. I should have guessed right off his relationship to the rest of the staff from the way that they laughed at his jokes— nervous, canned laughter. All at once *they* were the captive audience. The way students laugh for the teacher. Har har. This puzzled me, since I didn't think his jokes were so bad. He winced behind the smoke screen of his familiar cigar. But it was too deep for me, I was oblivious. Iris was the only one who guessed the significance of the fact: it meant that Zelma was a privileged character.

And she really was, too. An heiress, her family worth millions—stables, kennels, tennis courts, swimming pools. She insisted on preferential treatment: a room to herself, a TV by her bed, a car on the lot—all against the rules—and Dr. Lipman. (She had an analyst as well.) But Zelma protested so much about her privileged status here—here, where everything was upside down and inside out—that as a matter of course no one believed her. Only inmates like Iris and Zelma—power players themselves—instinctively grasped the hierarchy. They knew what was what. For what it was worth.

The long-awaited interviews took place in an adjacent new wing—construction had barely been completed. The walls were white with new plaster; glazier's marks were still chalked on the windows. Trespassing in these carpeted corridors, you glimpsed large conference rooms, deep leather chairs, polished tables.

Dr. Doremy's office, on the other hand, was a cubbyhole. No bigger than a filing cabinet; he rolled his chair out like a drawer. Iris was right; he lacked status.

Here—at last—the emphasis was on the individual. *I care about you.*

This was very much what you wanted to hear; you wanted to be convinced. But it was not convincing. The interns were just learning their creed. It was a lesson repeated in the classroom, a technique of the trade; a formula they had cooked up and were trying to dish out to you.

I care about you. I care about you.

You heard this now and knew you were hearing a lesson repeated, knew the doctor was just saying it, didn't mean it— didn't know what it meant. Here's hoping you might enlighten him. If you believed him, if he succeeded in convincing you, if he forced some confirmation from you—would that constitute caring? Yes, in a way. They seemed so anxious to see their formulas work.

"Now how about sex?" asks Dr. Doremy, clasping the edges of his steel desk and rolling himself up to it. His swivel chair keeps sliding away every time he crosses his long legs. "What is its importance to you in a relationship?"

I say it's really very important; but then again, it isn't everything...

"Okay. Good." Folding his arms across his narrow chest. "You understand about that then." We move on to the next thing. But such is the tempo of life on W-3.

The little room seems absolutely doused with light from the narrow window with its new pane of glass. It's as if a bucket of bitter gray water—one of the buckets of wash water always standing about in the halls—had been overturned and splashed all over us. I perch upright on a wooden chair. On the desk under my elbow sit half a dozen packets of tissues; the familiar little flat gray boxes you see all over the ward. And the gaping file drawer holds a ready reserve, contains nothing but a supply of tissue boxes. There must be nothing else in the whole damned desk. The place is flooded. The wastebasket is full of empties, balled-up tissues; someone has had a productive day. Lugubriousness, that seems to be the essential feature of the task at hand. I resent it, I hate it—I don't come here to cry! And yet I don't dare step off the ward on my way to one of these interviews without clutching the little gray boxes.

As a very small child I was taken to the Museum of Science and Industry. There were telephones there where you could hear the sound of your own voice; all you had to do was pick up the receiver and talk. When my turn came, I picked up the receiver and overheard someone talking and concluded it was me. So I hung up. I didn't understand how the mechanism worked, and it didn't seem so miraculous: If it could tell you how you sounded when you spoke, why not if you kept silent? The same voice. That's how I felt about the doctor's questions. Why couldn't he see into my head and read my thoughts—anticipate them? Why did I have to speak? What was there to say?

You? Who is this You? Is there a You? Who says?

I had a friend who was the son of a black sharecropper in Missouri. They had so many children they didn't know what to do. A neighbor came in one late winter night and found James and two or three others of the youngest children—one of them hopping around on a single crutch, for he'd lost a foot in an accident on the railroad tracks—putting on jackets and mittens, pulling woolen caps over their heads.

"Hey! Where you kids think you're going?"

James jerked a thumb at the ceiling. "Upstairs to bed."

James was a short, powerfully built man; he resembled Cootie somewhat, with his flattened features, his look of obstinate strength. All his family were the same. It was not until he had come up north on a football scholarship and gotten in with what he called "sportin' men" that James discovered he had had an older brother—the firstborn and bearing their father's name—who had been an up-and-coming heavyweight fighter in Kansas City twenty years before. The brother had fallen out with gambling interests, or so the story goes; his battered body was fished out, floating facedown in the Platte.

James had never heard the story or even known of such a brother. It had happened before he was born and was never spoken of in that house. There was nothing they could do about it. There are some things it's better not to talk about. What's the use? I understood the mentality; something similar happened in my family. My aunt was murdered when I was a very small child, a little more than two.

My parents owned a grocery store in the neighborhood and she was the one who used to take care of me during the day; I played with my cousin, a child of five. We discovered the body. My aunt had been strangled by a rapist, her apron strings knotted so tightly round her throat that they were hidden in the flesh. We thought she was fooling. We each took an arm and started dragging and pulling to make her get up. Her arm was limp and heavy, it offered no resistance.

A street of row houses, rooming houses, with long wooden steps; underthings drying on a painted radiator by the window; a yellowish linoleum with faded flowers. That was what she was lying on. A wooden ice chest stood nearby. I saw my father come rushing in, grab a bottle of milk out of the ice chest, and pour it out so it splashed all over her face.

The detective who worked on the case advised my father that the family should forget about it. They didn't have the money to pursue it, he said; it would just cause hard feelings. He must have seen hundreds of cases like that; it was advice kindly meant. And it was taken. My cousin moved away with her father and I never saw her again. The manner of my aunt's death was never spoken of in my family and I learned very early that the subject was forbidden. I kept my questions to myself. I could remember her dead hand pulling on me, and thought it was a dream.

After my first child was born, I had a howling postpartum depression and my husband sent me to a psychiatrist. After one session the psychiatrist told me (1) that I should watch television, "it's a good outlet"; (2) the only reason I wanted to be a writer was to control other people; (3) the dream that troubled me so much—the spilled milk—was an obvious sexual fantasy.

Not long ago I asked my father about it. He had been summoned from the grocery store just a few blocks away—the man people always ran to in trouble. He had picked his sister-in-law up and slung her over his strong back and carried her to County Hospital. But was there a bottle of milk? I asked. He winced with recollection. For some reason he had been told my aunt was poisoned, and when he saw her lying there he had grabbed up the first thing that came to hand—a bottle of milk from the icebox—and tried to force the antidote down her throat. It wouldn't go down, of course; instead it had splashed and run all over the dead woman's face.

When you left the carpeted psychiatrists' wing and returned to the more familiar, dingy, well-scrubbed corridors of W-3 (the mops and buckets and soapy gray water did not make it all seem less dingy), you would not be rewarded for self-discovery, individuality. It took no special knowledge to figure this out. Even a child will hide a sickness, afraid he might die. Even an animal. And instinct was backed up by the most practical considerations; you would be rewarded—that is, get out—only for taking on the same appearance as everything else. Merging with the surroundings. And that was the first impression you got when you walked onto the ward; that these shapes and outlines really had merged with the surroundings, become part of the furniture.

Everything here proclaimed the opposite: a fear of our reality, a dread of what was "right" for us, our "real" needs.

The thing that was never made clear to us on W-3 was the fact that the patients existed for the sake of the hospital, not the other way around. It was a conventional sort of mistake, and maybe the staff didn't quite understand it themselves. The lively packs of medical students with their tramping footsteps, their lab coats flapping around their ankles; the maintenance crews in their paint-spattered overalls, mounting ladders in our midst; the thin black scrubwomen in their dark-blue uniforms, thrusting their mops with such strange apathy; the clattering carts and piping intercoms; the laboratories, power plants, computers, generators; the hissing, leaking steam radiators (in the early mornings especially they sizzled and perked, as if the day were a broken-down engine that had to be repaired before it could get underway)—all this immense apparatus itself—this was the real life of the hospital. Once you understood this, it was simple, everything fell into place. Only it was the last thing that would ever occur to you.

The corridors were roped off; for two consecutive days they were waxing and buffing the floors and you couldn't hear yourself talk. We shouted over the noise at our meetings, made detours through the dining hall. Then some fault was found with the work; the wax had to be scraped up, the whole job begun all over again. The ward decamped, we all picked ourselves up and went in search of quiet quarters to hold our meeting. The motors whirred.

We were constantly being deposed. Elke's flaxen head bowed over the keys of the dark squeaky old upright piano, hacking out chords with stiff-spread fingers. "Those were the days, my friend, we thought they'd never end." Thump thump; her foot rocked the pedal. Her shoulders in her sheet-metal duster jumped with the rhythm. ("Taking out my aggressions," she called it.) She kept getting up to make way for the buckets and ladders.

"It's like living in a stage set," she remarked. "They're always shifting the scenery."

"Only we're the scenery," I said.

Gerda is hunched over, smoking; up to her chin in a bulky turtleneck, pale urchin head. Barefoot as usual—white humps and toes. She is clutching an ashtray in the fingers of her burned hand, the one thrust into its sleeve of cotton wadding. They are debriding the skin with a saline and antibiotic solution to minimize scarring. She begins to grind out her cigarette, heavy-lidded eyes downcast; spent. Like everyone else, Gerda is being fattened up, putting on weight. But the new flesh seems to find its way at once to the least resisting, the least defended part of her: her face. It's jowly; the cheeks seem swollen, packed in cotton, padded, narcotized—like someone who's just had a tooth yanked. The same look of dull misery.

All at once she stops, blinks, holding the still smoldering black tip of the cigarette; hefting the ashtray in her other hand. No expression crosses her face—it's trackless, a no-man's-land, it can't be traversed. But I am watching all this and it's as plain as day to me. Two alternatives have presented themselves to Gerda. She can grind out the cigarette against her flesh—where all those other scars came from—or she can heave the ashtray across the room. Try something different. The right hand and the left hand. Let us choose life. Okay, she heaves the ashtray. A perfunctory gesture; it shatters on the smooth floor.

The nurses observe this. No fuss. Folding their hooked rugs, stooping in their nylons to pick up the pieces. Someone is sent to fetch the broom. It's all right, no harm done; it's a good sign for Gerda. Jumping with a thrust of her shoulders, running off to her room on her little flashing white hooves.

Good, good.

As it is good, we are told, when we hear Charlotte weeping deep in her wheelchair. You can't tell who it is at first, can't tell where the sounds are coming from; they are so muffled, mewing, hidden—and yet they seem to carry all over the ward. Has someone brought in a child? Or a small animal—trapped somewhere? But it's so close, it could almost be within—coming from me, my own belly, the sounds I overheard during the night. I come out of my room to search for it: each time I have to find out for myself, have to locate the lost child all over again. The sounds are coming from that chair! Is there someone in it? Charlotte is so small she seems to be cringing inside. But these are supposed to be sounds from Charlotte—this is Charlotte's self weeping, the true sounds of her soul squeaking amid wired bones and spokes and tangled plumbing. Charlotte is an example for all of us. It's good; learn to cry, like Charlotte.

Back in her room, Gerda throws herself on the high bed, sobbing with frustration. She has broken the ashtray, nothing more.

No, this wasn't a good place to practice individuality, self-expression. You might end up expressing someone else.

Everyone was bound to fix on something with aversion, with childish fastidiousness. Disgust was a simple element of daily life on the ward—revitalized at every meal. The kitchen specialized in thin runny sauces that powerfully suggested the oozing matter in Gerda's burns, the snot dripping from Jesse's nose. You lifted your aluminum warming cover and wanted to put it back. Everyone had disgusting table manners, but some of us were harder to watch than others. It all depended. You would concentrate on a single characteristic: a drip, a leak, a lip. You couldn't stand the way someone ate, or someone else blew his nose, or didn't blow it. Those "accidents" when Charlotte's body fluids collected in puddles under the cranks and wheels of her chair. But it could be anything, anyone, any mortal secretion, any self-betraying trait. It didn't have to be reasonable. Or indeed, visible. The dreaded deadfall of Maurice's shuffling slippers.

For me it was the humps and toes of Gerda's tiny, distorted feet.

And yet she went barefoot, indifferently, almost brutally (it seemed to me) exposing them. Everything else was muffled, swaddled, and swallowed; she seemed wrapped in cotton wadding, heavy insulation, like the cast on her arm. She was always knitting, knitting, yards of bulky woolen sweaters—to pull over her head, on and off a dozen times a day. Her face emerging always with the same listless expression. That never changed. Nothing was exempt from the indifference in her eyes.

Drugs create this sort of indifference, but Gerda gave no quarter, she went beyond all bounds. What these bounds were, I don't know—but I recognized their absence.

It had happened again. I met Gerda coming out of occupational therapy, the bright whitewashed room. She was walking toward me with giant steps, one hand outstretched to show me her knitting. So it seemed. The face lifted, the chest rising, the arm floating upward on its gentle trajectory—it was like slow motion, a quick replay, a runner breaking the tape. I barely managed to realize that this truly was oblivion and to reach out and catch her before she buckled and swayed.

Gerda had tried suicide several time, had taken 112 Seconals once. Did she count them? But numbers always figure prominently in such tales; Iris's 27 years; Trudy had taken 117 of something; Zelma was partial to the number six, sometimes in multiples. She had been in a coma for 6 days; she got 600 cc of Thorazine in her buttocks every night. She took 6 Tuinals to get to sleep but didn't sleep a wink. Etc. Etc. She was still the most famous nonstop nonsleeper on the ward. There was no story without its numbers; you found yourself talking in numbers, numbers. *There must be some detail that is significant? Authentic? Maybe it's a number.*

All Gerda's stories had a rhetorical purpose anyway. In a hospital in Minnesota there had been "three Jesus Christs and a Mary Magdalene." There was a man who had murdered his wife, a mother who had slain "all" her children.

"My God! How many was 'all'?" I asked.

"All," Gerda repeated with a shrug, barely opening her little gill mouth.

There was no question about it; there was a sort of force field around Gerda that both pulled and repelled me. I hated to think what made her seek me out, why she had chosen to confide in me, what kinship she recognized. Her teeth were very tiny, steely, darkened with much dental work. Her mouth opened and closed very quickly, like a trap. Her voice was dim. It sounded weakened, exhausted, as if it had barely managed to escape.

In a hospital in Texas, Gerda had known a girl who kept threatening to kill herself; and that's what she did after they let her out. I didn't get the point of the story—light dawns slowly. The girl wanted to kill herself; she did. What of it? I couldn't understand why Gerda kept telling it, what she wanted me to feel for that unknown girl in Texas. A lurid figure, like one of my mother's vulgar divorcées. I didn't believe she really existed.

I knew that Gerda was talking about herself; that she was afraid *she* was that girl, that she would ask for help—was asking for it—and would not receive it. That was the meaning of the feeble glance, the cheeks with their dull tugging expression of misery. To suffer for nothing, for nothing—that is the real onus of mental illness. There were no numbers, no explanations. Nothing was real; nothing was significant. Only the madness she had seen in all those other places—authentic institutional madness—that was all she had to show for her suffering. She had been close to the real thing.

Vergil was in a catatonic state, a slender black woman in a bright-green dress. Her eyes were enormous, bulging like ostrich eggs. All her first evening, all through the night, she paced in the corridors with a timed, rigid step—thrusting her arms stiffly from side to side and snapping her fingers. She'd pivot about, swinging out her leg; her heels clicked in parade rhythm. Lying in bed you heard the clicking of those heels; and the clatter and roll—as of a windup toy drum—evoked the locked step, the big startling eyes of Vergil.

Some of us saw her, in fact; down at the other end of the ward she was propelling herself in and out of the rooms. The doors were always open.

My roommate, Kim, cried out in her sleep: No no. No no no. Tossing and farting under the blankets. I envied these unconscious noises. Sleep. Blissful, fitful sleep! Kim was a long-legged, delicate, reticent creature, her erect slender head wrapped in a towel; and she had a habit of lifting one leg, tucking it underneath her like a wading bird. So mornings she'd stand about on one foot and the other while I noisily splashed in the bowl and brushed my teeth, waiting to make her secretive toilette. All her habits were reclusive, self-effacing; I was scarcely acquainted with the sound of her voice, a high, nervous titter. She was a spinster in her forties and had been locked out of her apartment for nonpayment of rent. Same old story—but it had a new twist: her parents had persuaded the landlord to get rid of her. What's more, they had connived with ComEd and the phone company to get their service charged up to her too—sapping the very strength of the wires in her walls. She had proof—her utilities bills; she knew she could never have run up such whopping amounts. There was only one conclusion. The gods, her parents, the big power companies, were stealing from her. From Kim—five foot nine and eighty-seven pounds. Our vital statistics were measured regularly.

Kim hesitated to use the telephone, even here; our calls were free, but she was on welfare and didn't want to be spending "state's money."

Kim's mother, however, more than made up for it. When the old lady came to visit, she'd sit on the bed—a tiny black woman with a face like a wrinkled raisin sticking out of her babushka—and make phone calls one after another. Evidently she carried on all her business and social life in this way. That was the thing about the stories you heard on W-3; they always seemed too strange to be true, but there was always an element of truth in them. And in the end this grain of truth was all powerful—like faith in a mustard seed.

I worried about what fierce, lit dreams Kim might be protesting, lying against the wall. But I would have been glad to take my chances with dreams—listening to the sound of those heels clicking in the corridors.

Vergil was Georgia's new roommate; she kept returning to the room, pacing up and down between the two beds. Georgia was terrified, pretending to be asleep, the pillow over her head. Vergil would wheel about, swing out her leg, and disappear. Go after her? Suggest that she stop this pivoting and pacing and snapping her fingers? That, of course, was what you were supposed to do. But Vergil couldn't even see you; her eyes gleamed, they glowed in the dark, phosphorescent, like fish lures.

At last Georgia grabbed up her blankets and pillow and begged to be moved to isolation.

This continued; the next night, the next. On the third day, when Vergil finally did snap out of it, we were surprised to discover that the automaton all the ward had been afraid of was the gentle luminous-eyed woman in green, worried about losing her job in the cafeteria. (Few inmates seemed worried about their jobs, or to have jobs to worry about; they were almost inevitably black.) Vergil, for her part, was surprised to find herself on a mental ward. Now it was her turn to be afraid of us.

Afraid, but making allowances. You could see the same thing happening with her that happened with almost everyone; the bubble of lucidity surfacing. *Where am I? On a mental ward. Very well, that means that the rest of these people must be crazy. They may do strange things. So I mustn't be surprised at anything I see. And God knows I may see anything.*

It went something like that. This was the place where you expected God knows what. The trouble was, from everyone else, not from yourself. We could not understand the God knows what in ourselves, we could not make touch with it.

That was why we regretted seeing Frankie subdued, why we didn't really want to have Trudy hustled off and bundled away; that was the meaning of Julius's head banging on the walls of the locked ward. You could see the partitions trembling. The construction of the isolation cells was flimsier than any other on the ward, and obviously they were not always kept locked. What the locked ward was was symbolic. This was supposed to be a madhouse, wasn't it? It had to be somewhere, the raging in these walls? In there you could see God knows what. And we needed to see it; needed this expression, the alien, energetic, authentic forms of madness.

But what were all these doped, drowsy faces hanging over the trays at the dinner table?

Estella didn't eat with us. She was an outpatient, spending days only on the ward with her chubby baby; so big and healthy

in his crocheted little bootees and sweaters, his fat shoulders
like a football player's, that his bonnet strings disappeared in
the brown rolls of his chins. Her husband came to pick them
up every evening just at dinnertime. Rudolph would appear at
the pop of the buzzer signal: an immensely tall, black-skinned
man, thin, like an iron pike—striding quickly down the corridor
in his peacoat, buttoned to the eyes. He'd pop his head out
for a moment, inquiring at the nurses' station, then duck back
into his coat collar and go striding off down the other corridor.
You could already hear the baby's cries. It fussed and squalled
all the time, on its back, waving its arms and legs indignantly.
Estella could never figure out why he cried so much; there was
nothing wrong with him. He was big for his age, his eyes were
black and bright; he'd already been given his first haircut and
the back of his head, squared off, with its shaven neck, looked
just like a man's.

Rudolph would reappear with his son hoisted high on his
shoulder, bawling and kicking his bootees and fists. Estella
followed meekly, with a downcast gaze, clutching bags of dirty
diapers and clinking formula bottles. She avoided looking at
us as they passed directly in front of the tables. And Rudolph,
naturally he wasn't acknowledging any of this. He resented
Estella's "sickness," he was ashamed of it. Who would want his
child in this contaminated atmosphere? He jammed his face into
his collar and glared straight ahead while the baby shrieked on
his back—as if the father's grim, swift, long-legged steps were
snatching him vengefully from our midst.

No use watching Rudolph, following him with our eyes;
we wouldn't catch his eye, ever. But in that very gesture of
turning away, shunning us, fleeing the sight, we caught ourselves
most clearly. Sick people; weak, gloomy, repugnant, dragging
disgustingly at our food. Mental illness is suffering. If all the
rules and definitions were changed tomorrow, it would still be

suffering. If we were supposed to be so terrible, if there was something dark, demonic in ourselves—out with it then! What was it? For God's sake, where was its energy?

This was limbo. Who would not rather be in hell?

They wheeled in Mark, a big fair sandy heap trussed up in a bathrobe and propped in the chair. He had pneumonia, a temperature of 105; his large face had a stupefied, moronic expression—vacant with fever, with a growth of beard on his cheeks and mouth hanging open. This was not the drugged face that is fixed, preoccupied, the attention elsewhere. This was out-and-out slobbering. His breath was hoarse and panting and his eyes were a dull churning gray.

Gerda was temporarily evacuated from her room and they put Mark in the high hospital bed; pulled up the steel bars at the sides. On his back, spreading his arms and legs in the big crib, Mark called out: "Nurse? Water lady! Water lady! Nurse!"

Every once in a while this subsided, but footsteps outside the open door would rouse him again. "Hey lady? Are you the water lady? Water lady! Nurse!"

I looked in and saw his big head struggling shaggily to raise itself between the bars, his eyes turning dully toward the sound. He sank back again.

It was obvious he didn't really know where he was and all this must have seemed peculiarly indifferent to him. Such a constant procession of footsteps past his doorway, and no one to fetch him a drink of water? The nurses had told us not to. Even his breaking sounded thirsty; gasping, gulping—chugalugging— as if his head was in a pitcher of beer.

As a matter of fact, things *were* peculiarly indifferent. The nurses worked hard—but they were not solicitous, not here to fetch water. The astronomical fees did not include much that resembled usual hospital and nursing services, not what you anticipated. (It did include twenty dollars a day for psychiatric consultation and eleven dollars a day for occupational therapy fees—our yarn and beads. This last Gerda pointed out with particular bitterness; she was much preoccupied with what all this was costing.) "Do it yourself or go to hell" was the way Elke gently characterized the ideology.

But Mark was sick; he coughed all night. There was a fuse in his chest. A little black bomb. It was lit, it sizzled… it fizzled out. It was a dud. Lying in bed—undercover—I kept listening for the noise, concentrating hard for him: *If he could cough harder this time, if he could just get it out.* That was what he seemed to be trying for. Such an explosion would have been deliverance for all. But Mark didn't make it; he just kept coughing.

I was therefore surprised to see Mark making his way to the table the next morning—the big disheveled body lashing itself into a tartan robe. But everyone was required to put in an appearance at meals: Did I think they would send him his breakfast in bed?

What's more, it wasn't a matter of appearances; Mark ate like a wolf. As soon as he sank in his chair, he fell to, downing everything that was laid before him; without looking up, without asking questions—without breathing, it seemed. That heavy head didn't come up for air. This seemed strange to me, because the same head, with its coarse cheeks, loose lip, certainly raised some questions in my mind. Didn't Mark wonder—as I did— what he was doing here?

Several times, stumbling unexpectedly to his feet and shoving back his chair—muttering "Excuse me" (he seemed to address the chair)—Mark went crashing off to the water fountain, his feet sliding hastily in his slippers.

I found out that if you spoke to Mark you got the same results. "Excuse me." And back would go the chair, up would come the head, the open, alarming mouth—man overboard!—

and the big loose body would hasten away, clutching at its drawstrings.

We heard him splashing and panting at the water fountain.

Mark came to meetings. Same thing there. Sitting on the sofa with his hands between his knees. Knees, jaws, pajamas would start slipping, dropping open. The barometer was rapidly falling. His eyes were lobbing, gray as brain matter; his skull fluids were churning. If there was time, a hand would sway and paw at the air: "Excuse me." Exit lunging.

The fascinating thing about Mark at our meetings was that, during the five or ten minutes he stuck it out, he actually spoke. Contributed significantly to our discussions. Question: Ivan wants to start attending classes on campus. What about it? Mark raises his hand. "Ivan should be allowed to go to one class first, see how it goes. If all goes well, let him try another." Common sense. You can't beat that. Question: Yvette refuses to get out of bed in the morning. She won't get dressed the livelong day and eats nothing but chocolate doughnuts and popcorn. Any suggestions? Mark raises his hand. "Leave the poor kid alone. Just tell Yvette she can't come to the table if she's not dressed and then don't let her buy any more doughnuts."

What would you call this? There were plenty of others who appeared to be out of it and really were out of it; but Mark conveyed this impression more than anyone. He didn't know us, didn't speak to other inmates; he coughed all night, he raved with thirst. In the delirium of his high fever he found himself in a madhouse—what else could it be?—where, in his condition, he was expected to get up and come to meals, appear at meetings, attend to his own needs. His own consciousness was sporadic; as soon as he lay on his back it wandered off and we all became his passing phantoms. "Hey! Water lady! Nurse!" And yet now he spoke to these phantoms, delivered himself of his opinions. Breathing heavily; and when he finished speaking, his mouth would hang open, neglected, like a fat man's fly.

I don't know if anyone else found these outbursts of logic strange—these bubbles of lucidity. I was looking forward to Mark's recovery—the time when he would come to himself less intermittently—so I could start asking him questions. I was curious.

The fever broke, the delirium lifted—and Mark departed, leaving me mystified. Gerda returned to her high hospital bed, covering the listless route between her room and the table. She was its rightful occupant. No one disputed her claim.

I had good reason to be repelled by Gerda; she *was* my depression, the bottom of it—crossing the deeps, the rolling dark, that still lay ahead of me. I didn't need three Jesus Christs and a Mary Magdalene.

VIII.

On Halloween night I was given the task of serving, setting out platters of apples and doughnuts on crepe-paper-covered tables. When I came into my room to get dressed, Trudy was making herself up shrewdly in the lit mirror over the sink. She had established squatter's rights. On W-3 you always walked right in and helped yourself to what you needed, rifled lockers, pilfered from drawers; the place was like a fish tank, a balanced aquarium—nothing was ever lost or misplaced in this way.

Trudy looked around as I zipped myself up. "Oh, you finished your dress." I had been hemming this same beige jersey dress practically the whole time I had been in the hospital. Though I couldn't understand why it was taking me such a long time to finish it.

"Do you think it's even?" I presented myself, tugging and pulling at the hips.

Trudy shook her head. "I can't tell. Why don't you stand up on the chair?"

I climbed up on the chair, turning, trying to see the bottom of the dress and my legs in the mirror. Just then Inez's dark face appeared in the doorway; she paled, her long straight lashes swept up at me in alarm.

"Just what do you think you're doing?"

Jumping to my death, of course. I know that's what she thought. I laughed and climbed down, but Inez didn't think it was so funny.

"You better get dressed," she flung darkly over her shoulder as she went out the door.

I felt insulted, stung, downcast, gloomy. It was grim to be reminded of the sentence of death hanging over me. Because that's what it was, awaiting us all; we had a sickness people die of. And I felt particularly embarrassed in front of Trudy, standing there regarding me with her candid, penetrating gaze; the top of her blond head gleaming under the light. I ducked my head into the butcher's apron.

She sprang to my aid, taking up the apron strings behind my back. She drew them around my waist, held them fast.

"Hey, you're not going to try anything like that again, are you?" she asked all of a sudden. "Because it's not a good scene for you," she said. "For Zelma, maybe—but not for you."

I looked back over my shoulder. But Trudy had already bent her head, busily doing up a bow; her round cheeks hung heavy with dark powder. She had said this as she said everything else—because it was a thought that had popped into her head. But for me, it was the first message from out there—from beyond myself; I felt as if I had scaled a wall, glimpsed what lay on the other side. Not a good scene. Yes, I'll try to remember that.

"Listen." Trudy went right on as usual, without transition, taking hold of my arm. "I think my boobs are getting smaller. I want you to look and tell me what you think. Do you think it could be the medicine? Could it do that to me? Could it? Could it?" she insisted, hanging on my arm, pulling on me, trying to wrest an answer.

So she noticed it herself. It really did seem as if there was more to it than putting on weight; as if Trudy's body were undergoing some basic change, chemical, hormonal. As if all its natural processes had been reversed. Our life was full of such prodigies. It was commonplace, for instance, that women failed to menstruate; it seemed logical. We were exempted from the normal order of things. All claims had been superseded by the claims of this existence.

I didn't know what to think, what to say to Trudy. I felt that she had given me something and there was nothing I could give her.

Trudy's parents had at last sent her some clothes—all her clothes; everything (it seemed) they had ever bought for her; everything that had been hanging, unworn, unwanted, in the closets all these years; packed away in grocery cartons in the basement. Boxes, shopping bags, plastic storage cases; hangers, mothballs, mateless stockings; buttons, ribbons. Cheerleader fashions, bobby socks, pleated skirts, Peter Pan collars. Relinquished now, all of a sudden, as if they had finally conceded her loss; the loss forever of this Trudy, their Trudy, her pretty, blond childhood.

Everything was too short and too snug for her. Trudy rummaged with excitement at first (any sign of attention was so flattering); then with growing desolation. She paced up and down, swinging her shoulders this way and that, seeking something to try on next. Holding one dress after another up to her chin, gazing down at herself with darkening cheeks; flinging it aside on the bed. She'd outgrown them all. The austere little isolation cell was swamped with scorned possessions. It was the first sign of life out of her parents in all this time—they must have been busy the while with their housecleaning—and now they had responded with this overwhelming gesture. They'd gotten rid of her.

Trudy, the insatiable borrower, tried to give it all away.

She went peddling from door to door, bundles of moth-eaten, mothball-smelling stuff tucked against her chubby arm.

"Here. Take them. I want you to have them. They don't fit me anyway." Pressing, insistent, imploring as usual. Every day she delivered her bundles; every night the nurses rounded them all up and brought them back to her cell. And Trudy looked younger than ever now in her shrunken sweaters and short skirts, the snug little schoolgirlish clothes her parents had sent her.

Trudy and Yvette shared a crush on an inmate of the narco ward, the one who handled the laundry. The laundry chutes for both wards were in the short passageway between us, the dead end; a uniformed guard sat there inside a wired cage like a locker room; the inmates' belongings were kept in tagged metal baskets. But Trudy and Yvette kept the whole place under a surveillance of their own; they were always hanging about that door, watching and hoping for a glimpse of their friend.

My room was at the end of the hall right next to this door (which Maurice tagged regularly on his nightly rounds), and so I was privy to a great deal of this—the two girls standing there and arguing with each other, elbowing and shoving. They were constantly rowing; Yvette imitated Trudy, rivaled her in everything. Yvette had picked up all sorts of expressions from Trudy and would repeat them wickedly, not knowing what they meant; grinning naively with her little pointed teeth. Her voice was startling—deep, croupy, like a cough or growl. You'd look around to see where it was coming from. Her hair was kinky, reddish, albino red; her skin was white and rubbery, like an eraser; her lips were thick; her eyes were slanting, squinted.

"Why that's a mixed child, isn't it?" a visitor of mine had asked, eyeing Yvette thoughtfully as we sat in the lounge. I suppose she was that; I had never considered the question. What was she? Yvette was not a racial type at all; something else was going on here. Children with her troubles all have a family resemblance.

As soon as the other, the farther door opened, the two girls stopped shoving and turned with one motion, pressing their faces eagerly against the glass. The young man emerged in his striped bathrobe, swinging the lumpy laundry bags. Each, from its size and shape, could have contained a bound body. He was well built, heavy eyed, with a nylon stocking stretched and knotted over his slick, lacquered hair; it lay close to his head, smooth, like palm leaves. A guard moved quickly beside him.

The girls were knocking on the glass to get his attention, but he sauntered about his business, taking his time; tying the bags, dumping them down the chute. At last he caught sight of them—wiggling, grinning at him—and slowly approached the door. That was all right with the guard, who was leaning against the wall, grabbing a smoke.

The inmate fished a crumpled pack from his robe and extended it politely toward the bulletproof glass—offering the girls a cigarette. They shook their heads violently, delighted, watching him light up. They went on with their conversation in this way, grinning back and forth, gesturing in dumb-show.

What are you in for? Trudy signaled, cocking her head to one side. Yvette cocked her head too. He rolled up his sleeve, held his arm out to show them: muscular, fine textured, the dark skin satiny. Small raised scars like knots clustered round the veins. He gave his sleeve a shake and rolled it down.

And you? he asked in the same way, jerking his chin up and eyeing the two girls.

Trudy drilled a finger toward her temple: Ding-a-ling! They all threw back their heads and laughed—Trudy's blond hair swinging like golden chimes.

Brass bells! Tinkling cymbals! It sometimes happened like this. Admissions came in waves, in psychic currents; the ward changed colors like bubbles in a jukebox. Orange. Purple. Green. Now all at once it was full of teenagers.

This was originally Blanche's term. One night we'd heard her spreading the word that the ward was expecting a new admission—a teenager. Later on, very late, the whole floor was aroused by hoarse impassioned screaming. A new inmate struggling with the orderlies? The situation was common enough. Ordinarily, you couldn't make out the words, the particular passions of such outbursts. And these were loud and clear:

Let me out, let me out, let me out!

It was a warm night, the window was open beyond the big locked screen. I got up and looked out. A car had pulled up outside the emergency entrance, the curb where we waited for taxis. It was a late-model Cadillac, but it didn't sound so hot; its engine was knocking like eggbeaters on a helicopter. All the doors were open and you could see the passengers inside climbing over the seats. A woman lay beside it on the sidewalk, a coat spread under her and her apron front swelling like a wash basket. She must have been in labor; her legs were working, she kept pushing one out and dragging it in, tossing her head from side to side. She was the one who was screaming; powerful, throat-scraping yells. *Let me out, let me out, let me out!*

But no one seemed to be so much as looking at her. The others—the car was full—were scrambling to get their seats. The car took off while they were still scrambling, the doors swinging open. There was a screech; it stopped, it swayed up and down; arms reached out and slammed the doors. It struggled off in this way, braking and bumping without headlights in the dark. The woman still lay kicking on the sidewalk under the violet arcs of streetlamps.

Not everything that was strange was confined to W-3.

Kim had got up to look out too, standing beside me in her nightgown, one knee tucked under her. "I thought it was the teenager," she said.

It was what I had thought, what everyone thought. And it was prophetic. Now everything was "the teenagers."

There was a knock at my door. An unfamiliar face peeped round the corner, bright eyed and smiling. It was bituminous black, with slivers of green eye shadow over the eyelids; long rhinestone earrings, like pulleys, swung and sparkled from her ears.

"Hi. Y'all busy right now?"

La Donna slid round the door, tall and ladylike in heels, hose, white cotton gloves. I watched her speculatively, wondering what was going to turn out to be wrong with her. Buttons were missing at random down the slender front of her dress.

I cleared a place for my visitor to sit. I was unpacking some boxes and there were things all over the bed and chair. La Donna obliged out of politeness, barely perching herself on the edge of the chair. It was plain she didn't really want to sit; she was stretching her head eagerly, trying to see what was in the boxes. Even the big rhinestone earrings at her cheeks seemed to be quivering, brimming with curiosity.

"Don't let me interrupt y'all now, hear?"

I had packed these boxes myself when I was getting ready to move, before I had landed on W-3 instead. Now a few of them had arrived and I kept rummaging in them, looking for things to wear. The only items of any conceivable interest to me now, a pair of shoes would have been a boon. But I wasn't finding anything, and I was wondering where to put the boxes. The place was so cluttered up, it was beginning to look like Trudy's room.

"All these things yours?" La Donna asked, a little enviously, lifting her chin and glancing around. At last she couldn't restrain herself; she jumped up and began to poke in the boxes too, large bony wrists protruding from her soiled gloves.

"What's that, what's that?" she wanted to know.

A few get-well cards and family photographs leaned against

the shelf alongside the bed. La Donna fingered the cards. She picked them up; opened, scanned, clapped them shut. Not what she was looking for. She picked up a photograph.

"Who's that?" Pointing to one face and then another. I looked over her shoulder.

A photo had just come from Florida, my mother and father and the two boys on the beach. The sand was white, the sky was blue, and the sun must have been very bright, because they were all turning their faces aside and squinting. The younger one, slender, handsome, with his hands on his hips, ducking his dark head so you could see the thick whorls of hair. The older one, light haired, thoughtful, shaded his eyes. He'd had a lengthy illness when he was younger and I used to be afraid he'd turn out to be "sensitive." When he was very small, very towheaded, he used to seize people by the hand, kiss them, struck by some unexpected kindness. Once, when a bus driver passed me my change, my son—overcome with gratitude—pressed his lips to the burly hand punching out transfers. Now he was sturdy, broad shouldered, built like my father—whose hands lay protectively on the boys' shoulders, his big hairy chest pale under the brown circle of his neck.

"Those are my sons."

"Aren't they fine. You must miss them a lot."

But that wasn't it either. La Donna's eyes roved about under iridescent lids. She had spotted my roses. They were still standing on the desk, moldy stems thrust into a quart jar. The water was green, fishy, and the blooms dark as dried blood.

"Oh how beautiful," she whispered, sailing straight up to the desk and sticking her pretty, cheerful face into the dry petals and leaves. She sniffed and stroked.

"Y'all sure got a lot of nice things here," she sighed.

It was true. I was one of the lucky ones. I received cards, flowers, had snapshots to display. Loved ones to miss. My sons

were my home. La Donna's face among the flowers eyed me
with bright inoffensive curiosity:

"Y'all got a boyfriend?" she asked suddenly.

That was it—the signs she was looking for. La Donna only
wanted to talk about boyfriends; this was the major concern
of her life.

La Donna was what you call nubile; high breasted, buttocks
projecting, wagging walk. There was an onward, upward thrust.
("Hey can I step on those?" a man once yelled to her from
a—slowly—passing car.) She was another one whose parents
had dumped her bag and baggage on the hospital—too hot to
handle, I suppose.

She had a whole lockerful of clothes, everything in the latest
style, snappy stretch boots, hot pants, miniskirts. Everyone
borrowed from her. One size fits all! There was hardly a woman
on the ward who didn't take her turn; smearing her eyelids with
La Donna's thick pearly stuff, at La Donna's makeup mirror—
which lit up like a theater marquee. She was a godsend, generous,
the great benefactress of the ward. Her parents had also sent
her entire record collection, 45 rpms, which we could have
done without.

Now the roster was complete. Night and day we had revelry.
Yvette danced with La Donna, La Donna danced with Trudy;
Jeffrey beat his bongo drums till his fingers bled. Georgia's
portable record player sat smack in the middle of the table,
pumping out Herb Alpert and the Tijuana Brass. "Winchester
Cathedral." It was deafening, a form of brainwashing; the tin
covers hissed and rattled on the trays. Georgia liked her music
"*top vol*-ume." *Geor*-gia was *al*-ways *em*-phasizing. Peevishly;
glancing up from her work with hostile black eyes.

She was making a black-and-yellow rug in a design of
her boyfriend's initials. You had to pull each and every thread
through two holes in the canvas backing to form a loop; then

this loop was snipped, knotted, and snipped again. I never tried to make one of these things, it looked like maddening work. But Georgia went at it incessantly; steadily, deliberately—not to say vindictively—yanking the yarn with the little hooked instrument, digging in with the blunt-tipped kindergarten shears. Snip snip snip. "It *stead*-ies your *nerves*."

Her thin light face with its restive bones. The coffee-colored skin was all one even tone, pale and smooth; her eyes were long, dark, silky—they absolutely nestled in a bed of thick lashes. Her nose was chiseled, her cheekbones wide, her lips were full—why say more? Beauty is a gift like any other, and Georgia had it. When you saw her flowing into breakfast—in her empire-waisted robe of green velvet, with her swallowtail eyebrows and carbon-black hair—you were grateful, you didn't ask questions.

At nineteen already divorced; her baby daughter dead of lead poisoning; victim of gang rape, involving among other things numerous court appearances. She had moved and changed her name, so I'd heard whispered. She dragged the rug around with her everywhere; toiled at the table. Her lips whitening, tightening, as she dug in with the little child's scissors. "I don't *like* it here." Yank. "There are *too* many *meet*-ings." Knot. "It's all so *bor*-ing." Snip. She made it seem angry, bloody work.

But there was no getting away from that portable record player. Cha-cha cha-cha Cha! It could be heard at the farthest reaches of the ward. Callers would ask over the telephone what all the noise was about. "Oh, just some people dancing." Then Yvette went one better; she discovered the loudspeaker. W-3 was not hooked up to the paging system of the rest of the hospital, but we were wired for sound; the radio in the nurses' station could provide a sort of Muzak. Mercifully this had not been used very much, but now Yvette took over and played rock 'n' roll over the radio in loud competition with the Tijuana Brass sizzling on the table.

"Hey, what's the big idea! Shut it off and I'll kill you," Yvette would growl, rising, standing guard over her radio and folding her arms across her chest. Her eyes were like slashes; she was very big and strong. She walked on her toes. She'd come up and press herself against you: "Oh, I want to hug the life out of you!" Or, squeezing harder: "I could kill you." It was not possible to distinguish between her moods of murder and affection, and I don't suppose she could either. She wore a leather strap around her head like a ribbon, for she was always being nagged about her hair. The buckle was prominent in the middle of her forehead.

Yvette lolled in bed till all hours, though she fell asleep as soon as her chin hit the pillow, Deronda, her roommate, reported. "She must have a brick in there; she knocks herself out." She flirted with the busboys and medical students and the nurses took her to the canteen to buy doughnuts and popcorn— her chin was always greasy. She could stay up all night if she wanted to, play the radio whenever she felt like it, as loud as the spirit moved her. No one could tell her to stop. "No one can tell me anything. There are no rules here. You're no better than me. It's a free country."

Ha. It was better than that. You could have said it was a madhouse, if it wasn't a madhouse.

But it was Trudy who was the ringleader, the pacesetter, the flagship of the fleet. Yvette wasn't the only one who was copying her; all at once everyone on the ward was saying "no shit" and "fuck you"—even Dr. Lipman.

So it was announced. Trudy would be transferred to Idlewild, the state institution. The doctors said there were better facilities. But what did this mean, better facilities? More experienced doctors? The latest experimental drugs? More advanced techniques, equipment for confinement and restraint? (We had straitjackets too, and tables like the ones Trudy had been strapped down on at Tyndall. Trudy the veteran.) What it meant was, more simply, bigger. So big, in fact, so crowded with inmates like Trudy so much worse off than Trudy, that the shock waves she was sending all through our ward would be lost there in the general vibrations.

W-3 was not big enough for Trudy.

Trudy herself was flattered by the attention, being singled out in this way, made the center of special arrangements. And especially the interview. When she got to the state hospital, she would have to be examined by the board first, before it was official. This was the merest formality, but Trudy was very nervous about it. She was looking forward to it anxiously, flustered and excited. To her, the chief thing was the interview.

"What should I wear to the interview?"

"What do you think they'll ask me at the interview?"

"Tell me what I should say at the interview."

She seemed to think it was some sort of an audition, a starring role. It was practically the only thing she allowed us to talk about now, over our trays at the two long tables. But no one else was in the least bit worried about the outcome of this interview.

"Don't worry Trudy, you'll do just fine."

How could she miss? Lately, she had taken to wearing a long quilted robe, very demure like all her own clothes—tiny checks, lace ruffles round the collar and cuffs—but covered by now with all sorts of stains; smears, holes, cigarette burns; mustard, coffee, dried blood. On visitors' night Trudy dragged one of Jeffrey's friends into her room. Afterward she paraded down the corridors, leading her catch by the arm in his leather jacket and jeans; her cheeks besmirched with great red spots, and the front of her robe sporting a large fresh wet stain. Every visitors' night another boy, another stain—prominently displayed on the checkered robe.

"Just be yourself, Trudy," we told her.

Easy enough for us to reassure her! We weren't going to any interview. And in a few minutes she'd be at it again, desperately, leaning over her tray, a worried flush spreading under her cheeks: "Do you think I'll be a *success*?"

The doctors had told her that her examination before the board must be "successful"—i.e., Trudy must appear sufficiently crazy—before she would be accepted at Idlewild. That's just their jargon; it didn't mean anything. But it meant a lot to Trudy: she wanted to be a *success*.

The interview loomed so large in her head, she didn't seem to give the slightest thought to what lay beyond it—walls, gates; months, even years. Just as well. If she had asked about that, what could you have said to her?

Now finally at the last Trudy's stepfather put in his appearance; a fattish balding man with rimless specs, in a light-gray business suit. On visitors' night Trudy cornered him at the Ping-Pong table, dragging everybody up—he must meet all her new friends. We all had to be introduced to Father Bob— to distinguish him, rather reverently, from her other father, Father Jim. This matter of parents could have more complicated permutations; Yvette's mother had been married five times, like a movie star. And Trudy's younger sister, sitting at the table, wide and silent in her big poncho, was deaf and retarded. This red-faced, round-eyed man had bitten off a good deal when he married Trudy's mother.

He was surrounded, grinning, shaking hands, wildly ill at ease. "Here! Say hello to Father Bob!" Trudy yanked me by the arm. Father Bob was smiling encouragingly. Trudy had always been a peculiar child, always lonely—he didn't want to discourage her friendships. Not even these friendships.

"Trudy can be a little rough at times," he said to me, holding out his hand with a nervous laugh. In case I didn't know it. But his handshake, surprisingly, was a pull, a tug; and in the same way his eyes inside round fatty spectacles were trying to seize my eyes, hold on to them. As if to keep them from straying to the blond bell of hair, the characteristic squared-off, swinging shoulders—to prevent me from seeing Trudy as he saw her.

The strange thing was that this importunate, pleading gesture reminded me so completely of Trudy herself.

She was leaving next day; she opened her fist to show me the four sweaty quarters she was clenching. "Spending money. Father Bob gave me."

She would be off first thing, before breakfast, so now was the time to say goodbye. She went around distributing her bundles, very determined, as usual. "I can't take it with me anyway," she said, getting a little maudlin as her time approached. She was taking only a small suitcase with her in the morning; all the rest would be shipped off later—after the interview. She still didn't know what she was going to wear to the interview.

She lowered her face, bit her lip; her lashes sparkled.

"What is it, Trudy? What's the matter?"

"Never mind, it's all right," she said, grimly wiping her eye. "I always cry when I leave nuthouses."

During the night I heard someone knocking about, stumbling into my chair. It was stately Hazel, in her glazed white uniform, searching with her flashlight for the bundles Trudy had given away.

Next morning, I found Trudy in her long quilted robe leaning over the sink by the drinking fountain, trying to sketch a pair of eyebrows in the little gum-machine mirror on the paper-towel dispenser. It was very early; the hallway was still in gloomy darkness, the nurses were changing their shift. Smoking, carrying cups of steaming coffee to the nurses' station. Someone was tapping with one finger on the typewriter. It was the time of day that belonged to the hospital, mysterious as a submarine.

Dot was lounging in the lit doorway, arms folded, regarding Trudy with a skeptical eye.

"Time to get up, Trudy. Time to get going."

Dot was taking Trudy to the interview. She was the same nurse who had escorted me onto W-3, tiptoeing ahead with my roses in her arms. Tall, neat, with short blunt-cut auburn hair, a bit short and blunt in her ways. Always on duty. Elke said Dot reminded her of a Wren (Elke had lived in England after the war). And it was true, she always gave the impression of being in uniform.

Trudy's wrinkled clothes lay all over the bed. She hadn't even begun to pack. Now she fished around, picking one thing and another out of the mess, flinging it back. She didn't seem to be looking for anything in particular; seemed to be poking around absentmindedly, distractedly. Her blackened eyebrows— the only makeup she'd managed to put on—gave her white face a thickened, brooding expression.

I knew the feeling that had come over her: The moment of departure. *Something I've forgotten. Where is it? What is it?* But the soul has already taken off, light and swift on its journey. The body lags behind, vacated, deadweight, slow to move on.

I watched her stepping and turning about the room with her heavy tread.

Dot leaned against the door. "Five minutes, Trudy."

The next moment we heard her heels quickly rapping and she stuck her head back in with an inspired afterthought: "Your breakfast is getting cold."

I selected a dark-green sweater and slacks, some of the things Trudy had left in my room the night before folded on my chair. Trudy quickly pulled them on and looked down at herself. Too short, too snug, like all her clothes now; her stomach stuck out and the sleeves were tight on her pudgy arms. She accepted it. At the table she sat down and stared at her tray. Coffee, grapefruit, toast.

"Maybe you ought to eat something before your interview, Trudy."

It was the first time the interview had been mentioned today. She nodded and picked up the toast and began to chew. There was a lump in her throat. I watched her full cheeks munching, moving. I suddenly understood. Trudy really was a child. It was a chronological fact. There had been no time to grow up; she'd lost years of her life in this way. They were gone—how could she ever catch up with them?

Dot appeared in her coat, gripping Trudy's suitcase; she must have packed it herself. She set the bag at her feet.

"Well? How about it, Trudy?" she said, glancing down and slipping on her gloves.

Trudy got up at once. She was evidently relieved. Any departure was a kind of deliverance, and it went both ways.

"Call me," she said. "Come and see me." But she spoke automatically, without looking round.

She hoisted the suitcase and—just as she was, shrunken sweater and slacks, no hat, coat, gloves—hurried off after the sound of Dot's high heels, already rapidly departing down the corridor. Trudy doing her rugged best to keep up: her head bent forward, her shoulders raised, the short blond hair swinging from her white nape. The suitcase bumped against her leg with every step.

That same afternoon Sydney came up to me in the lounge with a gleeful expression on his face. His pink mug was leering. The way it leered when he stole the volleyball from Elke and me and dribbled away across the ruddy deck—shifting the ball from one hand to the other, hiding it behind his back, grinning at us, tossing his lank hair and rolling his eyes.

"Did you hear about it yet? Trudy's back. They're trying to keep it quiet. They've had her stashed away in isolation all day."

What—Trudy here a whole day and no one know about it? How could that be?

"It is! It is! I'm not kidding. They can't figure out what to do with her next. They turned her down at that other place, they sent her right back. She was too sane for them. Ho ho ho. Some doctors they've got there. Real sharp cookies."

And he bounced off on his elevator shoes to spread the consternating rumor.

But you could believe Sydney. He was trustworthy, wise, street-smart; he had a knack for picking things up. He'd never finished school, he'd dropped too far behind; he was supposed to be dying with kidney trouble. They had given him extreme unction when he was eleven. Sydney told me that he couldn't recall any fear of dying—only that the fuss distressed him. His mother's grieving face was embarrassing. He wished she weren't there. If she'd just go away and leave him alone so he could roll over in peace! That was all he wanted to do. But when Sydney shut his eyes and turned his face to the wall, his mother let out a shriek and threw herself upon his body. She thought it was the end. That was when it began to penetrate: the tear-streaked faces, the stultifying flames of the candles, the wailing and shrieking. He was the one who was supposed to depart. They didn't mean to go away and leave him alone after all; they had things backward, they wanted him to go first. He decided then and there not to die for them, and he held his ground.

That's the way it was with Sydney. He was an automobile mechanic, knew everything there was to know about engines; he'd picked it all up hanging around gas stations. Same way he'd picked up his skills at the pool table, just hanging around. The way he picked up everything. I often wondered what he was going to do, when he got back into the real world, with all the human insight he'd picked up on W-3.

If there was anyone who could get wind of a scandalous rumor or inform on what the doctors were up to behind our backs, it was Sydney. And he was right, as usual. Trudy really was back in her cell. She had gone off in such a chastened mood that she behaved very unexpectedly at the famous interview. You could see from the expression on the staff's faces that she'd fooled them too; they hadn't been expecting any such results. We'd all had such complete confidence in Trudy.

They were keeping her in her room until they decided what to do. But so far keeping Trudy quiet was not the problem. Trudy herself refused to come out to dinner; she was afraid to face us. She'd flopped, she'd been a failure. They didn't want her at the other place after all, and in the meantime she'd had a chance to figure it out—she wasn't wanted here either.

What was she up to now? Gulping bread and water in her cell? There seemed to be a new note of austerity, penitence even.

Once again all we could talk about at the two long tables was the interview! the interview! There was almost a buoyant, gleeful mood. The inmates were glad Trudy was back, glad she had put one over on the powers that be; the stern-faced examiners at the state institution. Not to speak of our own doctors, who had had the buck passed right back to them.

"Hang sending Trudy away," Pearl said, sinking her dark muzzle over her tray. "It's that Yvette they want to be getting rid of. Somebody better do something about that girl."

IX.

Once a month the externs on W-3 changed assignments and we got a new lot. I had come in just before such a turnover and now there was another; so I got to see at least a dozen, and they tended to have one feature in common. Boredom. It was the same with them as with the students I had seen standing stiffly around my bed in their white jackets. Or the dull yawning faces you saw when you went into classrooms to be interviewed. It was simple; it was all a classroom. Their presence was compulsory; we were here for their instruction. We were "teaching material."

Our externs had no specific duties in connection with us; we had no stitches to be removed, no bones to set; they couldn't peer at us through proctoscopes or poke our bellies. No ways they could make themselves feel useful. All they could do was relate to us; they too had to be out, out, out on the ward.

"It's just a waste of time as far as I'm concerned," as Seymour Sobeloff put it. Seymour, the most bored of all our externs. (He won hands down.) Seymour had short arms and legs, a thick body, a round woolly head that swayed from side to side as he walked—as if his cheeks were sagging under their own weight. He dozed off in the midst of meetings, his mouth stretched in a smile, his glasses beaming, fondly clasping his notebooks to his belly. Seymour was a lover. The first thing he did was show everyone on the ward the photograph of his fiancée he kept in his wallet (a redhead with a dark greasy chin), and the clipping from the neighborhood paper announcing their engagement. After that, there didn't seem much left for him to do, so he spent all his time in occupational therapy making an ashtray out of colored tiles. The design was a heart pierced by an arrow, displaying his and his fiancée's initials. Like Georgia's rug.

Seymour sat in a corner on a high stool, the ends of his necktie tucked into his shirt pocket to keep them out of the glue pot, smiling blissfully, indiscriminately—the way he smiled in his sleep.

This was the last place he would be likely to run into any patients. That was another of the peculiarities of life on W-3. OT was a bright, ample, whitewashed room, by far the pleasantest place on the ward—the only place where the windows were not darkened by bars or the overcast gloom of one-way mirrors. In the afternoon it was full of brilliant autumn sunshine. It smelled of paint, paste, sawdust, glue; there were deep zinc sinks and rough-hewn tables, and Lil—the boss—bustled about with great energy, a fringe of brown curls on her high forehead, her double chins shaking.

Attendance here was highly approved, received highest ratings. "They like it a lot if you show up in OT," I was told right away. And yet I never spent much time there. No one did; inmates stayed away in droves.

I remember the peculiar impression I received when I went into OT my first morning (starting out on the right foot) to see what it was all about. I sat down in my robe and slippers and began snipping flower petals out of crepe paper with kindergarten shears. My hands were trembling and my cheeks felt hot; I noticed this every time I bent over the paper; tremors of heat rose from it, it buckled and bubbled like tar.

Four or five other women had come in; I didn't know any of

them as yet, though the one with the red curls must have been Flora; and another was Simone, her eyes telescoped in her thick lenses. It surprised me when one by one each of these women did the same thing: threw down her work, burst into tears, and rushed out of the room. The nurses took off in pursuit. I kept on cutting out petals from red crepe paper, trying to steady my hands and get my eyes to focus. The heat was blinding; my head felt light.

But I was much more struck and more surprised by the strange goings-on around me.

In no time the room was cleared out and I was left alone with Maxine, the new assistant, a thin mousy girl with a large dripping red nose. Maxine had never worked in a hospital before and she caught every bug that made the rounds; she always got colds, she had no resistance. Indeed, I was to see very little of her later on, she was out sick so often.

She was sitting across from me, her nose stuck in a wad of Kleenex, the damp hair plastered on her face.

I whispered that I needed the glue.

The glue was at the nurses' station. "Go get it yourself," Maxine told me, glancing up dejectedly with watery eyes.

I couldn't resist it. I leaned over to whisper: "*I refuse to leave the room.*"

She clapped the heel of her hand to her forehead. "Oh my God. Six of them run away and this one refuses to leave."

So that's how I found out I was "one of them."

As with any other activity on W-3, most of the time was spent in rounding people up, trying to get them to go. Or, in the case of occupational therapy, to get them to come back. I didn't throw down my work and weep, but my reaction was essentially the same. I simply couldn't tolerate it. And I didn't know why; why I felt so restless, couldn't stay put; why I wasn't bent over industriously, gluing stones on key chains and painting numbered pictures. Even those of us who seemed able to attend to close work, like Georgia and Flora, who were always hooking rugs, apparently felt the same aversion to the room. The solution to this mystery was the same as the solution to all the other mysteries; but I could never understand it.

In the meantime all this was just fine with Seymour, nothing could have suited him better. He sat so contentedly, his belly easing over his belt buckle, gluing the little tiles to the copper form. He was the only one who seemed to find this sort of thing really therapeutic. But one day, alas, he was banished from his refuge; Lil got cross with him, rolled up her sleeves and turned him out. He wasn't supposed to be sitting in a corner, making ashtrays for his girlfriends; he was supposed to be relating, getting involved. Besides, she had a budget to consider and kept a tight hold on the purse strings; these were not the good old days.

Around nine thirty every night the kitchen sent up snacks—bologna, cheese, sometimes ham or turkey, orange juice, ginger ale. We made sandwiches. The turkey especially was really first rate—thick white breast slices, not stringy or dry, and the ham wasn't bad either. New inmates never took much interest, but those who had been around a while looked forward to this part of our routine, the most sociable activity of the day; we began to collect in the lounge when it was time—eyeing the big round clockface in the nurses' station and waiting for food.

Now, every night, just around nine thirty—you didn't have to look at the clock—who should come waddling in, as if by accident, hugging his books and wagging his cheeks from side to side? You guessed it. Sobeloff! (By now we were calling him, contemptuously, "Sobeloff.") He took a seat, glancing round, rotating his head; and it remained in motion until the food appeared. Then he fell to. Snapping open pop cans with a thick thumb, smearing mayonnaise, stacking sandwiches—a hand like a trowel. Three slices of bread at a time. Our ham! Our turkey!

Down the hatch. There wasn't that much. Not with Sobeloff around. His wide mouth smiled even as he chewed; this was the consolation he offered himself after his expulsion from OT with his fiancée's ashtray half-finished.

"I didn't get any turkey last night," Jeffrey complained at rounds. "And I like the turkey." Jeffrey was taking a radical interest in the food of late, polling everyone at every meal to see who had been shortchanged. He wanted to get up a petition.

"Me too!" I piped up. Various grumbles and murmurs. We were always ready to mount an attack.

"How come those big fat externs get to eat up all our food?"

Yes! How come? All over the room accusing eyes were turning on Sobeloff. He smiled at the ceiling, asleep behind his round glasses, rocking his books on his belly.

Actually, we were pretty hard on these externs; we were not easy to get along with, we were difficult. Easier to relate to abdominal hernias, broken legs. If they paid too much attention, they were meddlesome, nosy; if they didn't pay enough, then what was their excuse? There was no happy medium. Damned if you do and damned if you don't—that was our motto. It seemed to cover everything.

New teams of externs were introduced at rounds. Along with three or four young men in neckties and white jackets sat a young woman with black hair and black harlequin frames. Dr. Doremy felt prompted to ask if she were a patient. The young woman threw back her head and let out a shriek of laughter; light swayed in her glasses like chandeliers. The other externs—and most of our staff—laughed with her. Har har har.

Everyone knew what this laughter meant. It meant, I don't belong here! This was what every one of us felt, what we heard all the time, what almost everyone said—one way or another. Only none of us had ever laughed.

It was something of a relief when the old externs took their leave, when the new ones came in and took their places. But very quickly the feeling would spread among us that this new lot of externs was even worse than the last (if that were possible)— more deficient, unsatisfactory, lacking, disappointing.

It is not sufficient to be normal. There must be some redemptive quality in normalcy? We were seeking this special quality, we needed to see it, had to be on the lookout. This had become the real business of our lives; peering into mirrors, fretting over appearances, trying to get a look at it, find a glimpse of it somewhere. If something was wrong, then what was right? Would you know it if you saw it? Life on W-3 was exemplary. Those were our needs.

To the externs all the standards of the real world applied; they belonged to it, they represented it. The staff represented normalcy too; anyone did who came in from the outside— the cleaning women, our visitors, the busboys in the kitchen, shoving steaming steel carts. But they all had some other, more obvious business with us; and our visitors were not official. It was the externs, tossed among us by the stern, providing hand of the hospital, on its authority, who were really out on a limb. Their position was extreme: this was the one thing—all—they might have offered us.

The staff never seemed to realize that they were also under observation. People feel this sort of immunity with mental patients, children. I think this must be why I've had so little to say about the staff: because they had so little to do with it. They did not share our lot. In the end, it really was the inmates who mattered to one another, who made the only difference.

There were many moments that reminded me of childhood. What else could you expect? We behaved as children, we were treated as children, the offenses committed against us were the offenses committed against children—the same petty deceits. (Why did people keep talking to me as if I couldn't hear them?)

And it was understood that our very condition had something to do with childhood—the seething cauldron of all our woes. For our sins, we had been returned. We were as children. And our childishness was so much taken for granted, a shameful fact of our shameful lives, that it was a long time before I understood what it was really all about. That all these children within us were just our own lost selves.

Yvette. A most unavoidable presence.

Morning after morning she came stumbling into rounds, routed out of bed in her pink nightie—barefoot, rubbing her eyes, dragging her toes—like a Raggedy Ann doll with her raveled red hair. Knocking over lamps, ashtrays, upsetting piles of magazines; things tumbled in her vicinity, scattered and flew, she didn't need to touch them. She collapsed on the sofa, digging her fingers into her eyes, picking her toes. This was spiritual drudgery. She was our Caliban.

A voice spoke out.

"How come Yvette didn't comb her hair this morning?"

These remarks were always addressed at large, supposedly coming from all of us, emanating spontaneously and unanimously from the group. "Don't we think Yvette should be showing us more consideration?"

This was unfair. Everyone knew she'd only just got up; we watched her grooming herself. Besides, it didn't make the slightest bit of difference if Yvette did comb her hair; she was forever combing it. She bound it, oiled it—it would not be restrained. It kept sending out its signals: something was wrong.

Sometimes, for the sake of variety, Doris would speak up—casting sly glances into her lap. "I think we should compliment Yvette; it looks like she combed her hair this morning." (Hooray. How many points does Doris figure on earning for that one, I wonder.)

Yvette would look about, grinning naively as we discussed her, the tip of her tongue between her pointy spaced teeth.

Why isn't Yvette getting up on time? Why can't Yvette comb her hair? Why doesn't Yvette eat anything but popcorn and chocolate doughnuts? Why is her skin so greasy? Yvette! Yvette!

Yvette's lesser miseries were so numerous that you forgot the great ones; that she was mentally retarded, handicapped, epileptic; that her mother tied her up with strips of wet rag, beat her with brooms. From the first, the child had been ugly, clumsy, noisy, destructive—it knew its condition. Unloved, unwanted. The last act of tenderness the mother had shown Yvette must have been when she gave her her fanciful name.

Yvette was the only one who didn't seem to mind all these discussions; she'd never had it so good, never received so much attention as when we picked on her, nagged her, day after day about her hair.

"Yvette!" Pearl challenged one morning, drawing herself up haughtily to her full height (something less than five feet) and blowing out her black cheeks like a bulldog. "Yvette! What have I to do with you?"

A good question. Thrilling. I was impressed. It was bad enough having to put up with Yvette; why did we have to talk about her all the time? And yet we did have something to do with this strange child, that was the trouble, her problems were—eminently—our problems.

Some tried to show Yvette affection; Elke privately, Iris in public.

"I love Yvette like my own child!" she declared. At the next moment bursting into a dust storm of dirty-eyed weeping, mascara leaking like a squid, running down her cheeks— evidently shaken by the force of her own emotion.

Most of us were more like Pearl—puzzled by the presence of Yvette and the demands she seemed to make on our lives.

Eventually Pearl went after Yvette with a bread knife she had smuggled in for the purpose.

It was plain that Yvette—her proximity—disturbed everyone, even the staff. They felt it too. Her spirit possessed uncanny powers of making itself felt. Maybe they knew what was supposed to be wrong with her; but when it came to that disturbing sensation—the actual, physical, almost kinetic effect the presence of Yvette produced on anyone near her, on any object within reach (you'd have to see how teacups rolled when Yvette propped her elbows on the table; ashtrays erupted and sprayed butts all over; a spoon, a comb, would go clattering away from her, fleeing her, rolling like a ball—while she came tumbling after, toes curling, pawing)—when it came to that active, agitated element, so volatile, diffuse, free flowing at night—the thing everyone felt lying in bed—then the staff talked about her hair. It must be her hair. Send Yvette out to comb her hair.

We couldn't send Yvette away; we couldn't dismiss the thing she made us feel. I felt a disturbing kinship with her, some close and painful connection. Her soul was in transition, her spirit's sleep was ruptured. But in her it was raised to the umpteenth power; she possessed the power of the general. That was her curious gift. She was a picture of my soul.

Our graduate students, Ted and Fred, announced a special activity: in place of our regular patients' meeting, we were going to hold a mock meeting instead. We would all draw one another's names out of a hat and exchange our identities for the meeting. This was one way of getting around the universal mistrust of evening activities; Ted and Fred had been pretty discouraged lately with the turnout for rabbits and turtles. (Ted was nervous and slick, with a pestering little black mustache, he was always jiggling his knee up and down in his jeans. Fred was baggy and pale, with a halting limp. I couldn't help thinking of them as the rabbit and the turtle.)

There was some excitement as Fred passed among the crowded chairs, handing around the hat. That was because everyone was hoping to get the same name.

"I got it! I got it! I got the name everyone is looking for!" Sydney was leaping up and down, waving the paper he'd just picked.

He was shouted down. It was supposed to be a secret. So he retreated into a corner of his chair, arms folded, fists in his armpits—hiding his precious scrap of paper from prying eyes. But he couldn't conceal his satisfaction, looking around with a smug pink face.

Elke leaned over. "He must have got Trudy's name." Who else? That was the one name everyone wanted, the chance we were all waiting for. We'd jump at it. But I was well satisfied with the name I drew.

Ted dragged a chair out into the center of the circle and called the meeting to order. We were still waiting to see what was supposed to happen next; the nurses laying aside their scissors and rugs—their kindergarten props no longer in character. Ted stretched out his short legs, brushed his hair forward into his eyes, folded his arms across his stomach. There was a hesitant laugh as we realized that all this meant he was Jeffrey, our new chairman.

"Will the recording secretary please read the minutes of the last meeting?"

Flora was sitting next to me on the sofa, her head bent as usual over the hooked rug in her lap, and she didn't look up even now to see who would be imitating her. Her notebook was stuffed into the cushions between us. I picked it up and began to read aloud in a drawling voice, frowning and squinting over the pages:

"The meetin' was cawled to order by Jeff-rey our president.

At…at… I can't read my writin'. The meetin' was cawled…"
My eyes blurred with tears. "Ooo nooo pleeze I can't read this. I
don't want to read it. The words awl run together. I don't want
to be recordin' secretary. I want to gooo hooome." Letting the
notebook drop, wringing my hands.

Flora lowered her eyes to her work, the red curls springing
on the top of her head as she plucked away.

"Anyone else got anything to say about these minutes?"

"Gooo. Hooome. Oooo why won't they let me?"

"Then the minutes stand as read."

Jesse's billiard-bald head popped up, right on cue. The
old man had risen to straighten his chair. He lifted it up under
his arm and hauled it off to the other side of the room, bent
over crookedly, his long arm swinging. He turned it around
and sat down facing backward with evident satisfaction—the
cotton plugs in his ears. I wondered whose name he had picked;
whoever it was, goodbye.

Our mock meeting moved hastily to passes and privileges.

Basil's turn. He sat up, looking a little surprised. He studied
the paper on his knee, licking his lips under his thin mustache.
Then he fluttered his eyelids and flicked his wrists:

"Like I want to tell you. There's this flick I'm simply dying
to see. I can't pronounce the name, baby, but it's all about these
cats in a loony bin. Can you dig it? I always wanted to know
what goes on in them places…"

Zelma was huddled in a chair at the back of the room—a
cigarette between her fingers, hands limp in her lap. Withdrawn.
Gerda, probably, judging from the slump and the cigarette. But
there were five or six inmates like that currently; and of course
now their numbers were doubled. Zelma herself was getting
to be more and more like that these days; she had moved into
a new house, so to speak. No makeup, her face pale and bare.
She bit her nails. She was through with the seven suitcases at

last; now she wore nothing but a coarse woolen shirt, army surplus, the tails hanging between her knees. Her shoulders seemed hunched, submissive under the button flaps, and the drab color resembled her dragging streaks of hair.

There was a thud. Gerda had kicked out her chair. She stumbled over it, mumbling to herself, an unlit cigarette bobbing between her lips.

"I need a light! Someone gimme a light!"

She slammed through the room on bare white heels, her striped robe flapping.

"Do you mind? You're interrupting the meeting."

"Fuck you," Gerda muttered over her shoulder.

There were claps of delight. We all knew who she was! (So Sydney hadn't drawn Trudy's name.)

"Fuck your meeting, too! You can all go to hell, if you really wanna know."

She sat down, throwing open her robe, exposing to the hilt her skinny legs. As I'd seen them sprawling naked in the emergency room. The gesture struck me as genuinely obscene.

Trudy was watching this, fetching glances at Gerda out of the gleaming tail of her eye. She looked the way she had the night after the fiasco at Idlewild, when the nurses let her repentantly into our midst. The bedraggled scapegrace with hanging head, flushed cheeks. I hate to say this, but there had been a change in Trudy.

Inmates had formed a special committee on her behalf, drawn up rules of behavior. One set for Trudy, another for everyone else. Thus: Trudy was not to pull down her pants at the table. If she did, we were not to ignore it or approve. "It's not appropriate!" And so on. Zelma herself typed these lists in triplicate and posted them prominently in the dining hall. The community always closed ranks when it was threatened; we had united at last in our need to absorb Trudy.

Trudy didn't know what to make of it. She was intrigued by all the attention; a little wary of it. (The way she was looking at Gerda.) Then even the doctors got into the act; they had decided to put her on lithium. This meant a physical workup, blood tests and so on—more attention. The nurses busying themselves about her chair at the dinner table, checking her blood pressure, taking her temperature. Trudy looking on with tilted head, watching as the gray rubber cuff ticked and puffed on her arm.

"They're going to try and help me," she murmured indistinctly, the thermometer tucked under her tongue.

I didn't care all that much for Gerda's imitation; too lifeless, malevolent. She looked like a death's-head. But I had never noticed before how much the thrust of Gerda's shoulders— as with some sudden provocation, jolting her to her feet— resembled the swaying of Trudy's shoulders. Flinging themselves this way and that.

It was La Donna's turn next and she leaned forward, the rhinestone pulleys swinging at her velvet cheeks. She was wearing cut-down jeans, a blouse knotted about her bare midriff—which was smooth and flat as a plank (a wonder no one ever offered to walk it)—a towel piled high on her head. Her skin so black it was shimmering.

Once Dr. Zeiss, in an evil hour, had seen fit to question La Donna's mode of dress. Didn't you see anything *wrong* with it? Its *suggestiveness*? Its *brevity*? All that *eye makeup*?

Half the women in the room had been dressed the same way (more or less), wearing La Donna's makeup and clothes. We had gazed back at Dr. Zeiss uncomprehendingly, our eyes murderously outlined in heavy black paint. No, we didn't see anything wrong.

La Donna wiped a hand across her mouth.

"I'd like to par-take of some culcheral activity. You know.

Walk around a mew-zeem or sit around and listen to classikul music. Somethin' high-tone like that."

She shrugged her shoulders, blinked her lids with their frosty icing, grimaced, fidgeted, scratched herself. She kept wiping her hand across her mouth, stroking her jaw like a monkey. What was that all about?

Elke let out a laugh—the first to catch on to herself. She leaned forward too, blinking, puckering her white brows, nodding intently. It was funny that I'd never noticed that particular mannerism before, wiping her mouth, though I was closer to Elke than to anyone else on the ward. To almost anyone else, period, I sometimes felt—considering the present circumstances of our lives. Maybe that was why.

There were a lot of onlookers. Georgia had folded her arms, tossed her beautiful head—indicating she wasn't taking any part in this nonsense. Too silly. Flora leaned over her lap, snipping without interruption. Davy Jones looked as though he'd taken up his favorite perch in front of the television set; thick red neck, burly arms on his chest. He was sitting right across from me in his sunglasses with mirror lenses; the steely rectangles seemed riveted on his face.

Sydney got up to make his move. He shuffled across the room, bent over—bent almost double—one arm long at his side. He picked up an ashtray, set it down, stuck out a trembling chin, looking for another. He took his time, weighing each ashtray in his hand. He looked exactly like Jesse.

But just then old Jesse swung himself up; he'd taken it into his head to make off for the dining room. He started out, dragging his chair, his bald head thrust forward and his hand moving around in his shirt.

Sydney turned pink to the roots of his hair. He changed course, shuffling now toward the dining room, bent over crookedly, his arm loping and dangling. Jesse fell right in behind him. They hobbled about in the darkened room, in full view of the rest of us—Sydney picking ashtrays off the tables, Jesse dragging out the chairs. It was wonderful, you couldn't tell who was imitating whom. Jesse had suddenly decided to play himself and now we had two Jesses. Everyone was howling with laughter, but the two of them seemed stark sober—their gestures could have been made in the silence of a mirror.

Sydney was actually shaking with laughter; he trembled, controlling himself, holding it in. And this was the last straw, the perfect touch—it made him look more and more like Jesse, with his old bald head on its quivering string. As usual, you couldn't tell whether or not Jesse was aware of any of this. You could never be sure he wasn't in on it, wasn't turning the tables, pulling your leg. The tufts of cotton sprouting from his ears. He smiled to himself as he swung out the chairs, feeling his chest all the while for matches.

It was Flora's turn. She was still yanking at her rug. "I don't *like* the meeting," she snapped out all at once, tossing her curls and glancing up spitefully out of the corner of her eye. "They're *all* so *bor*-ing. It's *no fun*!" She dug in, her thumb hooked in her scissors. Even Georgia laughed, the characterization was so apt and unexpected and had taken us all by surprise.

In the discussion that followed it turned out that Davy Jones had drawn my name. That was what he was looking so mad about.

"Do her? No thank you!" he said. "I wouldn't even attempt it."

Davy was another one who was shipped off to Idlewild, but without fuss or fanfare; he left without saying good-bye. I was coming down the corridor from Dr. Doremy's office when I saw his broad back pushing its way into the elevator. His hair was clipped straight across on his neck. An orderly was shoving what looked to be a clothes rack—rows of hangers, plastic bags, shoe trees.

"Good-bye, Davy," I called out, in the nick of time, as the door was closing.

He wheeled around to face front. He was wearing his shiny sunglasses. The door glided shut. There was no flicker of expression across his chrome-plated eyes.

I don't know the powers and properties of lithium, but inmates looked upon it as a miracle drug. It was believed that lithium could do anything—calm the violence; appease the spirits; lift the fog, the terrible sentence hanging over you. The trouble was, this miracle worked only in extremis. To be helped by lithium, you must first prove beyond help. Those were the conditions; that was the only way it could come to your aid.

"I like to have that bottle of sleeping pills in the medicine cabinet," Gerda once told me. "It makes me feel safe. Then I always know there's a way out if it gets too bad. You know what I mean?"

I did, unfortunately. I was getting to understand her better and better all the time. And lithium was like the sleeping pills in the medicine cabinet: the final out, the ultimate disclaimer. It couldn't bring you back; it was only for the damned.

X.

I was approached in the hall by a black woman with shyly inquiring eyes; magazines under her arm, a bunch of flowers stuck in her glove: somebody's visitor. She wore a wig and a coat of rusty short-haired fur that was fastened with great hooks—like claws—and had definitely seen better days. The pelts were split. She asked if I knew anyone by the name of Bette Howland.

She was the aunt of one of my oldest and dearest friends, Odile O'Malley. Looking more closely into her face as she took off her coat and sat down, I saw certain resemblances: sharp cheekbones and especially the sidelong gaze. She was wearing an ill-fitting old-fashioned suit—a color I hadn't seen in years, it used to be called fuchsia—padded shoulders, a peplum. It was obviously a hand me down from one of the "madams" she had worked for as a cleaning woman, but her "families" had all moved away and now she was employed in the hospital cafeteria. She didn't mind the job, she said, that part was all right; what got her was all the money they withheld from her paycheck. Income tax, insurance, Social Security. She was bitter in particular about the Social Security.

Odile had moved away from this part of the country years before. We had met at college when we were both fifteen, on big scholarships, bright girls from the nether regions of Chicago.

Odile had lived in the Mecca, a block-long apartment building on the South Side, the most notorious, most mysterious location in all the Black Belt. No one knew how many thousands lived there; not the landlords, not the post office, not the police, not the workers from the welfare agencies trying to deliver their relief checks. Not even the rats knew. It was a whole slum in itself. Odile had a very vigorous idea of what she was getting away from.

Her Aunt Rose had never left the ghetto. The address she mentioned sounded in my ears like the name of a battleground. It was a battleground. Shots ringing out at night, cars screeching around curbs, sirens. Their wail carrying like breezes on the night air. There is always a smell of smoke; arson, gunpowder, do-it-yourself urban renewal. People are accustomed to trouble. Rose told me that that very morning, coming to work, a man had gotten on the bus shouldering, of all things, a scythe. The passengers right away started making room for him, and sure enough he turned out to be drunk. They rang for the bus driver to stop and throw him off, but the bus driver took one look around and hopped out himself. Then everyone else tried to leave, but the man stood staggering in the aisle with his scythe and barred the way.

One little old lady never budged from her seat. ("You could tell she was just a housemaid," Rose said. "She had her shopping bag by her feet.") She took a gun out of her purse and held it on her lap. It was no bigger than her hand, but the barrel looked like a fist. The man got off the bus.

Still, Rose didn't believe in owning guns. "I don't keep a watch or no rings either—they just take 'em from you." She told me she was studying tai chi chuan, some graceful art of self-defense. She lived with a sister who spent all her time sitting in the dark watching TV and hadn't left the house for years.

"She's too fat to leave now," Rose said.

She asked me what I was going to do when I left the hospital. I needed first of all a place to live, and I expected to look for an apartment in the neighborhood—the line of least resistance, in more ways than one. Rose, the experienced victim, gave me a parting word of advice, fastening up her big coat hooks.

"When they say to you, 'Just gimme your purse,' you just give 'em your purse, honey. Don't make no fuss."

It was a long time before I understood the significance of this visit.

Visitors were not encouraged on W-3, they were not a part of our lives; we were too busy for such intrusions. That is what was said. The truth was visitors were not good medicine. They weren't healing, they hurt; they reopened old wounds.

I had found this out for myself very early on, almost my first week on the ward, when a couple of friends dropped by unexpectedly. It was not regular visiting hours, what's more, it was time for dinner; but they marched right in with no trouble at all. "They must have thought we worked here," they said. And it was true, they looked as though they had some official status; social workers maybe, or medical students—two pretty, bright-faced, confident young women in short skirts, sandals, with sunburned cheeks. The weather was still like summer, and they had just been sunbathing. I was proud of my fine visitors; I felt that it was their world I really belonged to—before I had somehow slipped and fallen, dropped into this other place.

I couldn't understand what I was doing, on the wrong side of the fence.

I sat down in my room to entertain them after a fashion. But almost immediately Edith stomped up to the open doorway. She was a very pretty Polynesian nurse, with long swaying hair, but she never cracked a smile; and light as she was, she had a peculiarly heavy tread—her feet always sounded like marching boots.

"Come on and eat, your dinner's getting cold."

My friends said they were sorry they seemed to have come at the wrong time. But I urged them to stay. I was still very hoarse, could scarcely speak above a whisper, and my chest whistled when I laughed. I had occasion to notice this because all of a sudden I was laughing a lot—for the benefit of my visitors. These death rattles must have sounded catching. My arms and legs were covered with shocking purple bruises.

"Come on and eat, your dinner's getting cold," Edith announced, once again, standing in the doorway. I couldn't understand why she seemed so concerned about my dinner—I didn't care about it at all. But she kept tramping back and forth and making her announcement; you couldn't help listening for her wooden footsteps.

My friends were restlessly eyeing the door.

It was getting more and more difficult to carry on a conversation. So I tried harder, holding my end up, doing all the talking. In my horrible voice.

"Maybe you'd better go and eat," one of them said, getting up at last. Very ladylike; the bridge of her nose was freckled and ruddy, lighting up her China-blue eyes.

I saw them out. They glanced into the open doorways as we passed—rumpled, badly made bunks; fluorescent lights squinting hard over the dull smooth floors that always needed scrubbing. Estella's baby was squalling on its back and Estella was bending over the crib with diaper pins in her mouth. Tears flashed like the pins. Estella wept continuously; tall, bespectacled, deathly calm.

"Be my judge, be my jury," she had suddenly burst out once at team meeting, "What does it matter if I open my heart, open my flood of tears to you? It's Rudolph I must lie with in the dark. Rudolph is a locked man to me. I pound on the walls but I can't find the door. He won't open." There had been startled silence in the closed room. Sobbing and weeping we heard all the time—the lowest form of self-expression. Safe, encouraged. But we were not prepared for such eloquence, a genuine cry of the heart. So this is what it sounded like.

"I'd cry for them too," Elke said to me later, "if I could cry with such dignity."

Elke was another one who cried all the time. Silently, her shoulders shuddering. (Same way she laughed.) Defenselessly, without covering her face; humbly raising her eyes. I couldn't stand it. Her tears trickled down her cheeks and she made no effort to wipe them away. But she didn't mean to cry; she wasn't doing it "for them."

My friends were taken aback by the infant's cries. "Is there a baby here?"

The meal really was in progress. Knives, forks scraping the trays; odors of steam-table food drifting blandly above the two rows of bent heads. A tray was set before an empty chair. It was obviously my tray, my chair, my place at this sorrowful table. So this was what Edith had kept calling me out for—to come and join the spectacle! I felt as if my friends had actually seen me sitting there; and I suddenly saw myself too—my head bowed over a tray, loathing and loathsome, thickened, confused, same as all the rest. And none of us really knowing what we were doing here, why we belonged, how we had come to this.

I didn't speak as we moved toward the door. This was the low point of the day; the hour when offices emptied, lights were extinguished. The task forces laid down their arms and fled— the place was being evacuated. Deserted. Its fires were banked, its life was ebbing away. Any minute now the stark figure of Rudolph, swathed to the eyes, would come striding in and then even the baby's cries would be snatched away from us. The last sign of life. And now my friends were leaving.

The door opened with its pneumatic pop.

They must have seen how my mood had changed.

"It's too bad," my other friend remarked in her gentle, self-controlled voice—looking back with a smile as they stepped through the door—"it's too bad you've lost your sense of humor about all this."

Lost my sense of humor! That was a slice! It was an attack on the very citadel of self. Nothing at that moment could have seemed more cutting, wounding. Not after I had just put myself out to be the good hostess. A frantic attempt. Laughing till I coughed and cried. All at once I understood that I was not the best judge of my behavior. Am I so far gone, then, I wondered. But the truth is I had not gone far enough yet. Not nearly far enough.

It is not a grateful thing to visit a friend in a mental hospital. Most people don't even attempt it in the first place. Little by little you learn the basics; that the rules are there to protect you from the visitors. (Or, sometimes, the visitors from you. I am thinking of how frightened my children were when my mother brought them to see me. Hearing my voice whispering.) Gerda had requested not to see her husband; Sydney, his mother. Such requests were always granted. We had been transplanted; the hospital was our protector now, the ward had become our family. But I didn't realize to what extent this had come to pass until I started going out on my own, venturing beyond the halls of the hospital.

When you signed yourself out on a pass you were in effect signing an agreement to stay within the boundaries of the university campus; you were on parole. This rule itself was another relic of the past. At one time the campus had embraced a thriving community; but some years since the entire area had been bulldozed for urban renewal. It was radical surgery, cauterization; there were no piles of bricks or bomb craters and the green grass grew all around, but the neighborhood had been obliterated. There were no stores or business streets, and if you wanted to purchase anything—shoelaces for Sydney's sneakers, skewers for Zelma's wigs; I usually had some such commission—or go to a drugstore, a dime store, have a cup of coffee, look in windows, browse in shops, you automatically had to transgress. Everyone knew it; it was another rule that seemed to exist purely for the sake of being broken. The staff looked the other way, and each of us could decide for ourselves how far to go.

This sounds like a very trifling thing. But it wasn't. Not if you had been away from the real world for a while—as far away as you could get; under an enchantment. It had changed in the meantime; it had become an inhospitable and intimidating place. These first few expeditions were frightening. Uncertainty lurked everywhere; every corner was a decision, every step was a risk. And if you crossed a certain street, leaped over a certain invisible line, you were suddenly on your own; passing beyond all bonds of protection, striking out into the unknown.

On these expeditions I felt not only the ward but the whole hospital behind me, pulling at me always, the great pile of stone, the labyrinth, drawing me back to it with the force of its sheer physical mass. As the ant is attracted to the anthill, the bee to the hive; for all we know, the iron filing to the magnet.

I was standing on a street corner at a grimy business intersection—off-limits, of course—when a car nosed up to the curb and parked in a crosswalk next to a fire hydrant. A woman hopped out, leaving the motor running, and went tapping off in her foxtail stole. For some reason I stepped out in front of this car and waited in the middle of the street for the busy cross traffic. *A false step! What did you do it for?* Right away I was giving myself black marks for lack of caution; for deciding to cross the street, for not waiting at the curb.

As I stood there, pinned by cars, by indecision, I heard a woman's quick heels, a car door slamming behind me. I caught a glimpse of a dangling foxtail. Then a roar, a screeching crash.

The woman's car had jumped the curb, knocking over the large concrete planter on the street corner. It had contained a stunted evergreen. Now the big tub and toppled tree, the upturned heaps of dirt, lay on the spot where I had just been standing. Trash, gnarled roots, dead leaves—it looked like the mound of an early grave. I could see the marks of the tires where they had skidded through the moist black earth.

The woman didn't even look out the window to survey the damage to her fender; she just backed the car off as noisily as she had come—the whole front end smashed—and drove away. I crossed the street, shaken. For the first time I realized what a close call it had been for me when I lay unconscious with those pills.

One day I called and asked someone to visit me. I had not seen Jay for a long time. We had gone to college together, kept more or less in touch. He was an old acquaintance, never close, and I didn't really understand why I had called him of all people until I actually laid eyes on him strolling down the corridors of W-3.

I was in the kitchen, ironing something to wear at the last minute, and happened to glimpse him through the porthole as he passed. He didn't see me or turn when I rapped, but continued to make his way directly and purposefully to the little reception window at the nurses' station and stood there pounding on the bell with the flat of his hand. As if it were a counter in a bank or a hotel lobby. A small, dark, almost delicate man; a handsome wavy-haired type with tanned cheeks and graying temples. He wore a jacket of soft cream-colored wool, a sky-blue shimmering silk shirt; and he shot dark glances around him. It was Sunday afternoon, a time when the ward was generally gloomy; but today, for some reason, we seemed to be doing a lively business. You could hear the smack of Ping-Pong paddles, the balls clicking on the pool table. Both games were very popular with visitors.

Jay was in building and land development, a vice president by now; his firm closed deals on both coasts, he was away on frequent business trips, and whenever I called, his wife complained of his hours. I wasn't the only one who never got to see him. And yet this was the first time the facts actually registered with me, fell into place. It must have been the sudden, striking contrast; the discrepancies in our respective situations. I finally understood what had been escaping me all these years: my friend was on his way up in the world. He was a self-made man, a success. Entirely self-made; his parents had been the drabbest, narrowest type of immigrants, his two brothers were harmless, feebleminded, his sister had never ventured out into the world from the family home—a flat dark and unkempt as a sty in the shtetl. He had told me once—we were lying on our stomachs on the grass, studying for an exam—that his aim in life was to achieve mediocrity. He meant the mean—golden or not, as the case may be; to be average, normal; to accept the standard.

I was the one who was subject to scrutiny; but I found myself scrutinizing Jay very closely instead. I was testing myself.

Jay rarely had a day free for his family, but he had given up a Sunday afternoon to drive out—bucking traffic—and take me to dinner. And what an afternoon. Blue and russet colored, warm as summer; the air was sweet and gusty. But you could tell that it was autumn because the wind was blowing, blowing, everything was hurrying and scurrying away. The small leaves crunched underfoot as we crossed the grassy mall of the park to the car: here sheep had safely grazed; now nurses carried steak knives for protection in their shoulder bags.

The car was like a yacht; it seemed to roll gently beneath me as I slid over the leather. "Would you like to go riding around for a while first?" Jay asked, holding open the door.

I had signed myself out on a pass and immediately began to go into the technicalities governing passes…. His dark face grimaced as he walked around and got in.

He pushed a button. There was a hum. The top began to lift and smoothly fold itself back. "Where do we eat, then?"

Once again I started to say my piece.

"What difference does it make!" Jay cut me off irritably. "They're not watching you, are they? How do they know what you do!"

This was confusing. The most establishment of all my friends, and the first thing he wanted to do was break the rules! But we were going to have to break the rules in any case—unless he wanted to dine in the hospital cafeteria. That'd be the day. Sniff cooked cabbage? Eat off sticky trays? In his Palm Beach jacket and Duro shirt? He'd rather die first. I glanced at his frowning, swarthy-cheeked profile. Maybe he had reason to be disgusted with me? Maybe I was playing a sly game, like Doris?

We chose a restaurant in a nearby hotel, a steak house teeming with Sunday diners. Black leather booths studded with brass nailheads; candles in red brandy snifters glowing rosily on the white tables. The bartenders in their gartered sleeves and red vests bustled behind the padded bar. Photos, politicians and showbiz celebrities, all over the walls; hen scratched with autographs.

"Something from the bar?" the busboy asked, presenting menus. He cupped a match and lit the lamp.

"Something to drink?" Jay asked; attentive, like an interpreter, translating for me. "Order anything you like," he went on encouragingly. "Would you like a shrimp cocktail? And you'd better order a steak too—how about filet mignon? I'll bet that's something you don't get in the hospital!"

We'd had steak this very day; the first time since I'd been in the hospital. Everyone had ordered it; you could see people remembering this as they drifted into the dining hall—usually so indifferent: Today we get steak! As soon as Trudy had examined her tray she went back into the kitchen and came out carrying a stack of paper napkins. She wrapped her steak up in the napkins, took it in her two hands and began to wring it out like a dishrag, grease oozing and dripping from the thick yellow bone. Then we all began lifting our warming covers, inspecting our plates, and there was a wholesale embarkation to the kitchen for napkins. The table fell silent as we chewed the tough meat.

"Oh, you'd be surprised," I said, running my eyes down the long red menu.

Jay's dark eyes glowing in the lamp had barely glanced at his own menu; he clapped it shut. A small man settling himself at ease in the deep leather booth. He was used to such places, they were all alike; he already knew what was on the menu, what he was going to order, and what the food would taste like when it came. But he would never have dreamed of going to any other kind of restaurant; taking chances; he dreaded squalor. And I saw it would hurt his feelings if I announced that I had already eaten and ordered anything but shrimp and steak. He had his heart set on giving me a treat.

To be fair, Jay was always like this with me; he knew I didn't get out much to fancy places. (His wife didn't get out much either, with their three small children, but never mind that.) And luckily I had entered my final phase: I could eat anything, everything, whatever chanced to be put in front of me, it didn't make any difference. It all tasted about the same. I was never hungry, never full, and the food didn't seem to count; I wasn't gaining any weight.

The glasses were put on the table. We raised them. "Well here's to—here's to—" Jay began.

"Right," I said gulping my drink down with a toss of the head. I don't drink that often and I forget you're not supposed to do that. In fact, there was something deliberately crude in my manner.

Jay was regarding me in the candlelight.

"Do you always let them talk to you like that?"

"Like what?" I said.

"Oh come on, you know what I mean. Those snotty little nurses; they were treating you like a two-year-old. Why do you let them get away with it?"

I knew very well what sort of thing he was talking about, the tone the nurses so often took with us. What puzzled me now was that I couldn't for the life of me remember anything out of the way that had happened when I was signing out with Jay. The nurses had spoken to me just as they always did.

"That's what I mean, doesn't it bother you at all?" Jay asked, frowning again, dropping his gaze to the tablecloth. His eyes large, soft, glowing like a woman's—especially by candlelight. Especially with reproach. But there was a quality of coarse virility too: the dark beard glinting under the close-scraped cheeks, almost like gunmetal. Still, I couldn't help wondering if his feet touched the floor.

"You're the last person in the world I'd ever expect to put up with that crap," he said.

My friends have always had an exaggerated notion of my self-respect. It was never too nimble. But I was troubled; things seemed to be going badly with me. Once again I had been found wanting. Someone had patronized me, insulted me, and I had been slow to take offense. A malfunction of amour-propre.

Busboys were sliding their slim hips between the chairs, delivering sparkling water glasses, butter dishes, baskets of rolls. By now our table was getting so crowded that we were constantly shifting things about, making room.

"Who was that bizarre-looking girl with the long face, all the makeup?" Jay asked as I dipped my fork into little livid frozen shrimp on their bed of cracked ice. "It looks like a bad paint job."

Zelma had been discharged. But only a couple of nights later, as I passed an open doorway, I heard someone squawking my name; and looking around I saw—peeping timidly out from under the lifted bedcovers—Zelma's familiar, disheveled head. I stroked her hair. Zelma had been busted again; this solved the mystery of all her mysterious comings and goings; she always managed to get sent here instead of jail. Treatment for narcotic addiction was out; "I'm no junkie!" But she told me that next time she thought she might try jail just the same: "I'm getting fed up with this place." I said I didn't blame her.

But today it had been business as usual, the whole cycle beginning all over again. Even her boyfriend, Fowler, was back, sitting side by side with Zelma in the lounge, his ensign's coat with gold buttons and bright metal hair; holding her hand. Her face like a burst of rare plumage sprang vividly before me.

"Which one do you mean?" I said.

"You've got to be kidding! The character who was sitting on the couch holding hands with the pansy."

Ouch. Worse and worse—this was beginning to be distressing. Something else I hadn't noticed, hadn't figured out for myself. Though of course it was plain as day. And I realized that Zelma's special kind of desperation would always be a mystery to me.

"All right then, who was that blond in the wet bathrobe? Don't tell me you don't know. She said she's a great pal of yours; she propositioned me when you went for your coat."

Lithium didn't seem to be having much effect on Trudy after all. She was making up for lost time. No wonder the place had seemed so lively today.

"You know, if you keep hanging around that place—"

"I know. I'm liable to end up crazy."

"That's right. That's just what I was going to say."

"It's what everybody says."

"Well? So? I suppose it isn't the truth? Anyone would go off the rocker if they had to stay in such a place! I think I even would myself," he added gallantly.

I was applying myself steadily to the food, my only defense; fishing limp lettuce out of swampy salad dressing. But Jay had barely touched his plate; it wasn't what he'd come for. Now he shoved it aside and got down to business, laying his cream-colored sleeves on the table.

"Look here. Just when are you thinking of getting out of there, anyway? It's about time, I'd say. You don't belong there."

I laughed; he looked hurt. But how could he know that this was only the universal protest? I'd had to fight it down—do battle with myself—and now he was bringing it up all over again. And I was shocked to realize all of a sudden the degree of my own success; how much I really had become of, one with, W-3.

"But look what I tried to do," I said.

Jay brushed that aside; a crumb on the tablecloth. "That doesn't mean anything; that could happen to anybody. You were physically beaten down, that's all. But you've got no business sticking around there now, when you've recovered your strength. The next thing you know they'll have you hugging yourself in a straitjacket; they'll cart you off to a padded cell. They'll convince you something's really wrong with you. Just a bunch of people sitting around, feeling sorry for themselves! Who cares about them! You're not like them. Why, you have more brains in your little finger…"

I was in for it now; I was going to hear the whole thing. So this was what he'd given up his Sunday for—to come all the way out here to give me a pep talk. And I knew it by heart.

After all, I'd given myself plenty of pep talks.

Life is so beautiful, we owe it so much... your whole life ahead of you, everything to live for... Bach, Beethoven, Michelangelo... (When you start dragging them into it, you're really in bad shape.)

I was not displeased, after all these weeks on W-3, losing myself, to hear a friend expressing admiration, flattering opinions. Telling me that I had been in the right all along, that the doctors were bungling and the nurses were stupid. I didn't really think this was so but kept my mouth shut without too much of a struggle. No, it didn't displease me. I'd forgotten how it felt. And Jay was really sincere; there was a light in his eye. I knew he'd had some private illumination of his own. He belonged to a success club, self-motivation, free competition, that sort of thing; he played records to himself in front of the mirror every morning the way other people stand on their heads or jog up and down the rug.

But I sensed something wrong with such arguments now. They were irrelevant. I had almost died. That was the indiscreet and undisguisable fact. It was vividly before me: the funerary heap of dirt and leaves from that overturned planter. I had almost laid myself down in my grave. Where were all these good opinions then? What use had they been? What difference did they make to me?

The gist of all the pep talks is that you can help yourself; you can straighten up, buckle down, fly right. But what if there comes a moment when you can't? And that's the moment you have to be prepared for. Pep talks are no good then. There's no use arguing with the enemy—the enemy has arguments of its own. More tender, more persuasive. They come to you as your thoughts; they speak to you as friends. They whisper, they infiltrate, take up their positions in the dark. Not a shot needs to be fired.

Suddenly I understood what Gerda had been trying to tell me all along. The girl in Texas—the unknown voyager who had gone ahead of us. She didn't really want to commit suicide, that was the point of the story. Nobody really wants to; I didn't want to either. There is nothing sacrosanct about suicide. Those thoughts that had come between me and my pillow were not my own thoughts—they were an enemy occupation.

"I'm afraid I won't be able to help myself," I blurted out, suddenly interrupting him. Jay looked at me with his mouth open.

"You can't say that!" he said. "No, you can't say that! That's a cop-out. That's just refusing the responsibility."

"It's not a cop-out." I leaned forward fiercely, fists on the table. I shook my head, unable to go on and explain. But I knew that I was right, that this was the only way of taking the responsibility, that I had only just now grasped my true situation. You can't take up arms against the outer darkness. You can't rely on self, on argument, on rational persuasion. There is only one thing you really need to know. That it isn't yourself. That the force is the enemy's. That you are alone, helpless, hiding your head—but that you don't want to die.

"Dessert?" said the waiter, sticking the menu in front of Jay's nose. He reared back his head to look at it; I think he's getting farsighted. Nothing for him; but for the lady, strawberry shortcake.

The waiter withdrew. Jay watched his retreating red vest. "You have to leave all this behind you now," he said. "You have to make a fresh start."

"I'm tired of leaving things behind me," I said—still in a charging mood.

But I had mistaken his drift. The pep talk was not all Jay had come to deliver; he had something else on his mind. He and his wife wanted me to come and stay with them for a while. Three children and one on the way, but they had talked it over and would love to have me. Now that he had seen for himself what kind of place I was in, he was more determined on this plan than ever; I must get out of the hospital as soon as possible. "The sooner the better," he said.

He didn't add, now that he had seen and talked to me.

And, in spite of everything, the curious glance he was continually throwing me, it still had not occurred to him— and the thought could not occur, there was no time for it, no room for it, it was not dreamt of in his philosophy—that there might be anything wrong with me. Anything I couldn't handle, that is, if I just put my mind to it... But I had to entertain this idea now, very seriously.

Jay's visit from first to last was an offer of friendship, and I was observing him to the most critical degree. I know that. But I had to be vigilant. His attitude was one of the most difficult things I would have to contend with in the future—in others, in myself. I recognized that now. I felt myself on guard, armed to the teeth.

Meantime Jay looked on approvingly, watching me dig into whipped cream, dripping red strawberries.

Dinner was over when I signed myself in, but Inez had kept my tray for me in the refrigerator.

I hadn't seen Gerda all that weekend; apparently she had had another seizure. I found her sitting on her bed, cranked up, propped against the pillows, knitting away in the dark with her big wooden needles. They were thick around as clothespins. I asked if she wouldn't like to come out and knit in the lounge. She nodded at once and slid off the bed and began to look for her sweater. Not that the climate in the lounge was any different, but this was the usual procedure; it seemed she couldn't leave without her sweater. And she couldn't find it either, casting about a spent, sleepy glance.

A large, dark, dumpy woman was sitting in the armchair, her fingers laced over the bulge of her stomach. She wore a housedress, bobby socks and gym shoes, and her hair was characteristically disheveled. She was sitting on Gerda's sweater.

"This is Margaret," Gerda remarked, tugging negligently at the sleeve. And Margaret nodded and smiled and eased up on one hip so the sweater could be slid out from under her.

No sooner had we arranged ourselves on the sofa in the lounge, with the balls of yarn and Gerda's needles clattering like sticks, than I noticed Margaret sitting across from us in a lounge chair, smiling amiably through the spaces in her teeth.

"She seems awfully attached to you," I said to Gerda.

"She's my nurse," Gerda replied.

Gerda had been on a one-to-one, twenty-four-hour surveillance. I had been on such an arrangement myself, what seemed long before, when Henrietta was my nurse. I didn't ask what Gerda had done this time, and she didn't volunteer the information; but all the same she seemed more communicative than usual. She explained that Margaret was a practical nurse: "They're cheaper." She was always ready and willing to go into financial details; after years of sickness, half a dozen hospitals, a dozen different psychiatrists—not to mention neurologists, various brain tests—mounting debt was uppermost in her mind. It was the foremost fact of her marriage; almost like something she and her husband had acquired together, like furniture, books, travel. Children. Gerda clung to the hope that there was some neurological, physical, even chemical basis for her illness—the thing I would have dreaded most in the world.

She moved her lips with some difficulty, the corners of her mouth tugging at her numb, paraffin cheeks.

"They're talking about putting me on lithium."

"Do you want it?"

She shrugged indifferently. "If it's going to help."

I knew what she meant; that she wanted matters taken out of her hands.

My friend Jay was right; it was time for me to leave. But not for the reasons he thought—putting it all behind me. This time I would have to take the long way home. But I had achieved my aim, got myself where I wanted to be. Not in a mental ward, that wasn't the goal; but free—free of my own personality, my particular history. Not so private, particular, and personal after all. Now I was ready to reclaim it—though it could never be of as much interest to me again.

I easily (since I took the very first one I looked at) found a flat in the neighborhood; Elke and I went out on our passes to clean the place up. She "took out her aggressions" on the blackened stove, scraping away in long rubber gloves; blond, intent. It helped. But even so, the place seemed rattling, empty, gloomy; it clutched at my heart every time I walked through the door. As if I knew all I would have to go through there yet. The worst part was still ahead. My sons would be coming back from Florida after they finished the school semester. I bought three beds and gallons of white paint—like someone laying in for a siege—and prepared to move.

One night a friend and her husband came and helped carry my things to the flat, and the next day—in the beige jersey dress, legs smooth shaven in nylons—I sat and listened to my last meeting. Dr. Lipman announced a change in policy; from now on new patients would no longer be required to introduce themselves to the group—they would not be put through the old routine. It had not "worked out." For me, this seemed a fitting ending—a closure of sorts; as if I had seen some change accomplished. And if on the ward, with its unwieldy weight of collectivity—then perhaps in me? And yet I am sure that it was not all of us who protested—each according to our ability; tears, hostility, silent withdrawal—who had made the real difference.

Iris had probably had more to do with the abolition of this practice than all the rest of us put together. She had demolished it. Too late for my benefit—but things always improve when you take your leave.

But I was wrong, it wasn't over yet; there was something that still bound me to W-3. Even after Elke left—I saw her off in a rush in a cab at the station—the place still had some hold, some unfinished business with me.

From time to time I received phone calls from Gerda.

She would get out a few muffled words in her thick, slurred, sluggish voice—a quality even more evident over the phone— many pauses, lapses, absences between. Or sometimes it would ring and there would be no one there. Holding the receiver to my ear, I could hear a long, struggling silence.

"Gerda? Is that you?"

Shouting into the empty telephone, as though she couldn't hear me. Maybe she couldn't; maybe she'd dropped it. She was still under surveillance, on very heavy sedation, and not allowed visitors. I was not so sure she was allowed phone calls either.

"Come and see me," her voice murmured.

"Then you can have visitors?"

"No. Don't." There was a stumbling click. I got the impression someone had taken the telephone away from her and hung it up.

Some days later I went back for a visit.

A black boy, very snappily dressed in stack-heeled boots; wide, cuffed trousers; and a split-skirted military greatcoat, was arguing with one of the nurses. Just as I got out of the elevator, she had slammed the door in his face and he was pounding the glass.

"I want my woman! That's my woman you got in there!"

A thin, fair girl, very plain, with narrow glasses and hair all skinned up in pin curls, pressed contritely against the other side of the glass. Her Kleenex squeezed in her first. Her tongue on her lower lip. Disconnected. This Unit Is Not To Be Used As a Thoroughfare, said the sign stenciled on the door.

"Gimme back my woman!"

The boy must have been all of sixteen. A steel comb stuck straight up in the back of his hair. The shoulders of his coat were stuffed, upholstered; he hulked under its dramatic weight. It looked like a burden. I really expected him never to leave, but almost at once he turned on his heel and knocked off toward the elevators. Two big sparkling teardrops rolled slowly out from under the prim specs and down the girl's pale cheeks. The tears struck me; I knew they had come from very far off.

Down the length of dim corridor behind her, through the window of the nurses' station, I could see the nurses' heads bent over their ledgers and the dark outline of an inmate in isolation, watching them through the glass. I knew who this was—a very young black girl with a close-cropped head, round nubile breasts. She wore a shrunken doll-size sweater. She seemed to materialize—a dark brutish outline against the lit glass. Her eyes were round and black as bull's-eyes in a target. She had just given birth; where was her baby?

At first she had kept trying to break out. You'd hear the noise, the thrashing footsteps. You'd know right away something was up—no one ever ran on W-3. She was making for the door, her head down, clasping in her arms her small bundle of possessions. But the door was locked. Footsteps were scraping behind her. She'd turn, looking this way and that; where to hide her bundle now?

The solution was simple. They took the bundle away from her. She still broke out, but now she only went from room to room, stripping, tearing, turning out drawers. And once she had emptied the clothes from the washer and laid the wet-licked litter in the middle of her bed.

She seemed permanent, a fixture. But that was always the first impression. I was struck now with the thought that immediately enters the head of any visitor: how was it possible to have spent any time at all in such a place, how could my soul have borne a minute of it? And I had thought that things had changed! Now I saw my error: the place was immutable. Things were always changing, things were always the same.

"Gerda isn't here anymore."

The nurse, sticking her nose out the door, seemed very anxious to close it on me. "She's over there now," she said, pointing down the other hall. "You'll have to ask at the desk."

I passed a row of swinging doors, glimpsing conventional hospital rooms, high white beds, aluminum bedpans and trays. At the desk a nurse in the usual uniform told me that Gerda was out—she'd gone for a walk. I was relieved. So all was well. I had had the feeling, passing all those doors, that I was walking steadily into a trap, that something was lying in wait for me. I didn't really want to see Gerda, I didn't want to see anyone. I had come as a duty and now it was dispatched—I was getting off very easily. I wanted to get out of there as fast as I could, get far away from that place, run for my life.

I punched for the elevator. Far down the corridor a white-trousered attendant was pushing a long empty cart strewn with bedsheets. The bell rang; the red light—for down—lit up. Something made me look again. The cart was not empty. The pile of laundry was a form, a body. It was Gerda. She really was as white as a sheet.

The nurse's starched cap lifted behind the counter. "Oh, here she comes now," she said.

Slowly the cart approached, creaking gently; sundry upended bottles splashing and swaying. This was what I had wanted to run from—turn tail and flee.

Margaret, Gerda's practical nurse, had a crony in the hospital who was looking after a man with a dislocated hip on the fourth floor. Every day when she took Gerda about the corridors for her walk, they used to stop up there and visit with Margaret's friend. One day Gerda found an open window and jumped out of it. That part wasn't really so hard to imagine— it was a gesture I'd seen her practicing plenty of times. Violent, almost perfunctory; that fling of her shoulders. There was something flat about her face now lying against the pillow; blue-lidded eyes, an odd cosmetic effect. Chalky knuckles.

"Nice of you to come."

Right away the attendant asked me if I'd mind "keeping an eye on her for a minute" while he went off to get something. As if she really were a bundle of laundry. Gerda was still under surveillance, even though—as she told me ironically—she had broken both ankles and punctured her insides and couldn't do herself a mischief if she wanted to.

"Oh yeah? Don't give me that. You could always figure something out—you're very resourceful."

"I just did it to get out of there, you know that, don't you? I thought they'd never let me out."

Of course I knew. That was what had always horrified me; and what made me seek her out too. We understood each other—to the limit. She was like a victim in the terminal stages of an illness; wasted, emaciated, no longer wanting to talk to the living—healthy, normal, callous types—the nurse behind the counter. The attendant with his hairy arms, leather straps on his wrists. She had nothing to say to them. Only to me.

The attendant gripped the handles of her cart. I knew that I would never return to W-3. Never, not for any reason, not to browse, not to visit, not to refresh my memory. And not as a patient. That part was over and done with. It was as if she had cut the cord for both of us. I felt drained, shocked—as if I had taken that jolt too.

Gerda was also leaving the hospital; as soon as she could get about on crutches she would be transferred to Idlewild. "I think it will be much better there. Anywhere's better."

She knew I wasn't coming back anymore either. We said our good-byes and wished each other good luck. I bent over the cart and planted a big red kiss on her cheek and we parted forever. On the way home I was sick under a tree planted in the sidewalk cement.

It was simple. I was afraid; I didn't want to die.

Once the lines are drawn, once you have recognized the enemy and called it by name, it shows its true face—it pounces on you, bares its teeth, claws with all its savagery. It attacks like a mountain lion. Night after night, as soon as the lights were out, the darkness went on the move; it rolled past me like a landscape—rough, hilly, thorny with underbrush. On and on it went, no lights, no clearing, I felt its breeze in my face. I thought this must be the valley of the shadow of death. I knew that I was moving through panic and terror—a state, a territory, a place on the map; and if I started struggling and thrashing I might never get out. And it wasn't the thing I was most afraid of. No matter what happens, there is always a worse fear: that you're losing your mind.

That was the fear that was closing in on me. I was alone with my children. Every night after I put them to bed I would start painting walls—staving it off. Was it happening again? Was the nightmare beginning? What if I got sick again, had to go to the hospital—what would become of the little boys then? I stuck the roller on a broomstick and slapped the white paint on in dripping coats while the sweat splashed down my face. The flat seemed very bare with its brushes and paint cans, rags, ladders.

My older son was lying on my bed in the dim light, digging his fists in his eyes.

"What's the matter?" I cried, dropping down and crouching beside the bed.

"I'm worried about you," he said, looking not at me but up at the ceiling and fighting back his tears with dignity. His wrists, his fists, were dimpled, round, and thick—a child's hands. "I'm worried that you'll get sick again, and then what will you do? If there's no one to help you, then who will take care of us? And what if you're left all alone?

I laid my head against his high, ribby chest. "Oh dear heart, I was just worrying about the same thing," I said. "So, you see, I'm not alone."

One day some months after I had left W-3 for good it all of a sudden occurred to me—I had had what is called a breakdown. That was what had happened, but I didn't know it. That is, I believe, one of the characteristics of the condition. By then I had moved on into other regions, and the word held no special terrors for me. In other words, it might also be described as a place.